Built from Breakdown

Built from Breakdown

Matthew Petchinsky

1

Built from Breakdown: The Collapse Code
By: Matthew Petchinsky

Disclaimer

This book is intended for **educational, informational, and personal development purposes only**. The content presented in *Built from Breakdown: The Collapse Code* reflects the author's perspectives, interpretations, and conceptual frameworks regarding personal collapse, psychological stress, resilience, adaptation, and transformation. It is **not a substitute for professional advice, diagnosis, or treatment** of any kind.

Nothing in this book should be interpreted as **medical, psychological, psychiatric, therapeutic, legal, financial, or professional advice**. The author is not acting as a licensed physician, psychologist, psychiatrist, therapist, counselor, attorney, or financial advisor. Readers should always seek the guidance of qualified professionals regarding any physical health conditions, mental health concerns, legal matters, or financial decisions.

This book may discuss themes including—but not limited to—**burnout, stress, trauma, breakdown, loss, collapse of identity, emotional distress, neurodivergence, disability, chronic illness, poverty, systemic pressure, and personal adversity**. These topics can be intense or triggering for some readers. **Reader discretion is advised.** If you are currently experiencing severe emotional distress, thoughts of self-harm, or a mental health crisis, please seek immediate support from emergency services or a licensed mental health professional.

Any strategies, frameworks, exercises, metaphors, or conceptual "codes" presented in this book are **theoretical and reflective in nature**. Results will vary widely depending on the individual. The author makes **no guarantees** regarding outcomes, success, healing, financial improvement, emotional stability, or life transformation. Application of any ideas from this book is done **entirely at the reader's own risk**.

This book does **not promote self-destruction, harm, or reckless behavior**. References to "collapse," "breakdown," or "burning down old structures" are **metaphorical and symbolic**, referring to internal psychological patterns, belief systems, identities, or life frameworks—not literal or physical actions.

Personal anecdotes, illustrative scenarios, or examples—if included—are shared **solely for conceptual clarity and narrative exploration**. Any resemblance to real persons, living or deceased, or to real-life situations is **coincidental or generalized**, unless explicitly stated otherwise.

The author does not assume responsibility for any actions taken, decisions made, or consequences experienced by readers as a result of engaging with this material. By reading this book, you acknowledge that **you are solely responsible for your interpretations, choices, and actions**.

This work is offered as a **framework for reflection**, not a doctrine, belief system, or guaranteed path. Readers are encouraged to think critically, adapt ideas responsibly, and disregard any concepts that do not align with their well-being, values, or circumstances.

By continuing to read *Built from Breakdown: The Collapse Code*, you acknowledge and agree that you have read, understood, and accepted this disclaimer in full.

Introduction: Why Breakdown Is Your Upgrade Sequence

No one prepares you for the moment when the system fails.

Not the quiet kind of failure—the kind that looks like exhaustion you can't sleep off, pressure that doesn't ease when you comply, effort that no longer produces results. The kind where everything you were told *should* work suddenly doesn't. Your routines glitch. Your identity lags. Your nervous system overheats. You feel like you're falling apart—and everyone around you keeps insisting you just need to try harder.

This book begins there.

What you've been taught to call a *breakdown* is not a personal defect. It is not weakness. It is not failure of character, discipline, faith, or intelligence. It is a **system overload event**—the moment your internal architecture can no longer support the demands being placed on it.

And that moment matters more than you've been told.

Modern culture treats breakdown as something to suppress, sedate, shame, or erase. We label it dysfunction. We rush to "fix" it. We try to return people to the exact structures that broke them in the first place. Productivity must resume. Normalcy must be restored. The system must continue.

But systems don't break randomly.

They break **when they reach the edge of what they were designed to survive**.

Your mind is no different.

A breakdown is not the opposite of progress. It is **what progress looks like when an outdated version of you can no longer run the current reality**. When the operating system you've been living on—built from survival habits, borrowed expectations, trauma responses, and social programming—can no longer handle the load.

In technology, when a system reaches this point, engineers don't blame the hardware. They don't shame the machine. They don't tell it to "push through." They initiate an **upgrade sequence**.

Human beings, however, are taught to panic.

We are told to fear collapse instead of decode it. We are taught to view exhaustion as moral failure, emotional shutdown as weakness, dissociation as laziness, and resistance as pathology. We are encouraged to override warning signals instead of listening to them—until the system crashes hard enough that it cannot be ignored.

This book exists to say something different:

Your breakdown is not an ending.

It is a signal.

And signals are information.

When your life begins to fracture—when motivation dies, identities unravel, coping mechanisms stop working, and the old scripts lose their authority—it is because your internal system is attempting to reorganize itself around a truth it can no longer suppress.

Breakdown is what happens when the false structures finally lose power.

This does not mean the process is gentle. Upgrade sequences never are. They involve instability, uncertainty, fear, grief, and loss. Old processes shut down. Familiar narratives dissolve. Relationships strain or rupture. The future becomes unreadable.

But inside that instability is **precision**.

Your mind is not randomly self-destructing. It is **deleting corrupted code**. It is rejecting frameworks that once kept you safe but now keep you small. It is refusing to run programs that require self-erasure, chronic compliance, or endless self-betrayal.

What feels like collapse is often **the moment you stop being compatible with a broken system**.

This book will not ask you to romanticize suffering. Breakdown is not something to seek, glorify, or manufacture. But if you are here, chances are you didn't choose it anyway. It arrived because the cost of staying the same finally exceeded the fear of changing.

The Collapse Code is not about "getting back to normal."

Normal is what broke you.

It is about learning how to **read the architecture of your collapse**, understand what failed and why, and rebuild from the inside out—not as a repaired version of who you were, but as an upgraded form capable of surviving reality without self-destruction.

You will not be given platitudes.

You will not be told to "think positive."

You will not be pushed toward artificial resilience.

Instead, you will be taught how to:

- Recognize breakdown as a **threshold**, not a verdict
- Identify which internal systems are obsolete
- Stop fighting the signals your body and mind are sending
- Extract power from instability instead of fearing it
- Build structures that can hold *who you are now*, not who you were forced to be

This is not a promise of ease. Upgrades require downtime. They require dismantling. They require courage.

But they also bring **clarity, precision, and strength that did not exist before**.

If you feel like you're falling apart, you're not alone—and you're not broken beyond repair.

You are in the middle of an upgrade sequence.

And this book is your guide to surviving it—without returning to the version of yourself that couldn't.

Chapter 1: Fracture as Function

The Myth of Malfunction

You were taught that when something fractures, it has failed. That cracks mean weakness. That continuity is strength and interruption is danger. This belief runs so deep that the moment your life begins to split—emotionally, mentally, structurally—you assume something has gone wrong *inside you*. But fracture is not always malfunction. In complex systems, fracture is often **information**.

Biological systems fracture to release pressure. Geological systems fracture to redistribute stress. Technological systems fracture when legacy code can no longer integrate new demands. None of these fractures are moral failures. They are responses to load. The problem is not that the fracture exists—the problem is that we are taught to panic instead of analyze it.

When you experience a psychological or life fracture, it is rarely random. It happens at precise fault lines: where expectation exceeds capacity, where identity contradicts reality, where suppression has replaced processing. The fracture appears because the system is trying to prevent a more catastrophic collapse. It is choosing a controlled break over total annihilation.

The myth of malfunction tells you to rush toward repair before you understand what broke. It tells you to restore the old shape at any cost. But restoring a system without understanding *why* it fractured only guarantees future failure. The same stress will return. The same load will be applied. The same fault line will split again—often deeper.

This chapter asks you to suspend the assumption that something is wrong with you. Not to deny pain, but to **reframe its meaning**. The fracture is not proof of inadequacy. It is evidence that something has exceeded design limits. That matters.

Once you see fracture as function, shame loses its grip. You stop asking, "What's wrong with me?" and start asking, "What is this fracture trying to protect me from?"

Stress Is Not the Enemy

Stress has been mislabeled as a toxin when it is actually a signal. Acute stress sharpens focus. Chronic stress, however, is not a failure of resilience—it is a failure of structure. When stress becomes unbearable, the issue is not that you are weak, but that the system you are operating within is unsustainable.

Your body and mind are not designed for indefinite output without recovery, choice, or meaning. When those conditions are violated long enough, stress stops being adaptive and starts becoming corrosive. At that point, fracture is not rebellion—it is *regulation*.

Stress fractures appear when the system can no longer dissipate pressure through normal channels. Rest no longer works. Motivation disappears. Emotions flood or shut down. You may dissociate, freeze, or burn out entirely. These are not signs of laziness or lack of discipline. They are emergency responses.

The tragedy is that modern culture interprets these responses as personal shortcomings. Instead of redesigning the system, it pressures the individual to endure more. Push through. Cope better. Optimize harder. The result is not strength—it is fragmentation without meaning.

When fracture occurs, it is often because your internal system is attempting to force a redesign that your external world refuses to allow. Something inside you knows the current configuration will not survive long-term. Stress becomes the messenger. Fracture becomes the escalation.

Understanding this shifts the goal. You are not trying to eliminate stress entirely. You are trying to **build a structure that can metabolize it without breaking**.

The Precision of Breakdown

Breakdown feels chaotic, but it is rarely imprecise. If you look closely, you'll notice that not everything collapses at once. Certain roles fail first. Certain beliefs crack before others. Certain relationships strain while others remain intact. This selectivity is not accidental.

Your system fractures along the weakest or most overburdened points—not because they are inferior, but because they have been carrying too much for too long. The caretaker identity collapses when it has absorbed everyone else's needs. The achiever identity collapses when worth has been tied solely to output. The compliant identity collapses when self-erasure becomes intolerable.

This is how you know breakdown is functional. It targets the structures that can no longer be maintained without harm. It spares what is still viable. Even in collapse, there is intelligence at work.

Unfortunately, people are taught to mourn the loss of these identities instead of interrogating them. "I used to be so productive." "I used to be so strong." "I used to be able to handle everything." What's missing from these statements is the cost. What did it require you to ignore? To suppress? To sacrifice?

Breakdown is not asking you to abandon strength. It is asking you to **redefine it**. Strength that requires self-destruction is not strength—it is a slow-motion failure mode.

When you stop trying to resurrect what collapsed and instead examine *why* it collapsed, you begin to see the logic. And logic restores agency.

Fragmentation Is a Map

Fragmentation terrifies people because it feels like loss of coherence. Thoughts scatter. Emotions contradict each other. Identity feels unstable. But fragmentation is not the absence of order—it is the presence of **multiple unintegrated truths**.

You fracture when parts of you have been forced into silence for too long. When compliance has overridden authenticity. When survival strategies have outlived their usefulness. Fragmentation is what happens when suppressed data finally demands attention.

Rather than asking you to "pull yourself together," fragmentation invites you to listen to what was split off. Each fragment carries information. Anger holds boundary data. Grief holds attachment data. Exhaustion holds capacity data. Numbness holds overload data.

Ignoring fragments does not make them disappear. It drives them deeper, where they exert influence without context. Integration does not mean forcing harmony—it means allowing each fragment to be seen, understood, and recontextualized.

The map of your fragmentation shows you where adaptation failed. It highlights the cost of pretending, the toll of endurance, the damage of chronic misalignment. This is not pathology—it is feedback.

Once you treat fragments as messengers instead of enemies, coherence becomes possible again. Not the old coherence—but a more honest one.

Collapse as Refusal

One of the most uncomfortable truths is that breakdown often contains an element of refusal. Not conscious rebellion, but an embodied "no." Your system stops cooperating with demands that violate its limits.

This refusal is frequently mislabeled as laziness, depression, or lack of motivation. But what if it is discernment? What if the part of you that shut down was the only part still capable of protecting you?

Collapse is sometimes the only language left when subtler signals have been ignored. Boundaries spoken quietly were overridden. Exhaustion was dismissed. Emotional pain was minimized. Eventually, the system escalates.

This does not mean every collapse is righteous or clean. Refusal can be messy. It can arrive as apathy, anger, or confusion. But underneath the chaos is a simple truth: something was no longer acceptable.

Recognizing refusal within collapse restores dignity. You are not weak for breaking. You may have been **stronger than the conditions you were placed in**.

Refusal is not the end of responsibility. It is the beginning of redesign.

From Repair to Rebuild

Most people approach breakdown with a single goal: fix it. Return to baseline. Restore function. But repair assumes the original structure was sound. Rebuild begins with a different question: *What was this system never designed to carry?*

Repair patches cracks. Rebuild redesigns load-bearing elements. Repair seeks speed. Rebuild prioritizes sustainability. Repair restores appearance. Rebuild changes architecture.

If you rush to fix yourself without understanding the fracture, you risk rebuilding the same failure point. True recovery is slower, quieter, and less glamorous—but it lasts.

This chapter is not asking you to celebrate collapse. It is asking you to **respect it**. To treat it as a diagnostic event rather than a verdict. To extract information before imposing solutions.

You are not here to become who you were before. You are here to become someone who does not need to fracture in the same way again.

That is the function of fracture.

Exercises

Exercise 1: Fracture Mapping
Purpose: Identify where and why your system fractured.
Steps:

1. Write down the first area of your life that noticeably collapsed (work, identity, relationships, health, motivation).
2. List the responsibilities or expectations tied to that area.
3. Identify what you were suppressing to maintain it.
4. Note how long those suppressions lasted.
5. Write one sentence beginning with: *"This fractured because…"*

Exercise 2: Stress Load Audit
Purpose: Understand what exceeded your capacity.
Steps:

1. Divide a page into three columns: Required, Chosen, Absorbed.
2. List stressors you were required to carry.
3. List stressors you chose to carry.
4. List stressors you absorbed from others.
5. Circle the items that felt non-negotiable but were never actually sustainable.

Exercise 3: Fragment Dialogue
Purpose: Reconnect with a split-off part of yourself.
Steps:

1. Choose one dominant emotion from your breakdown.
2. Write a question to it: *“What are you trying to tell me?”*
3. Write its response without censoring.
4. Ask: *“What do you need that you didn’t receive?”*
5. End with: *“If I listen to you now, what changes?”*

Journal Prompts

1. What was I praised for that ultimately broke me?
2. Where did endurance replace choice in my life?
3. What warning signs did I ignore before fracturing?
4. Which part of me collapsed first—and why that part?
5. What does my exhaustion reveal about my values?
6. What expectations am I still trying to meet out of habit?
7. How did I benefit others by breaking myself?
8. What would sustainability look like instead of recovery?
9. Which identity am I afraid to let go of?
10. If this fracture were intelligent, what would it be saying?

Closing Reflection

Fracture is not proof that you failed to hold yourself together. It is proof that you held too much for too long without the support, permission, or structure required to survive it. When you stop treating collapse as a flaw and begin reading it as feedback, something shifts. Shame loosens. Curiosity replaces panic. You realize you are not standing in ruins—you are standing at a redesign point.

This chapter is not about fixing what broke. It is about honoring the moment your system refused to self-destruct quietly. That refusal is not the end of your strength. It is where a different kind of strength begins.

Chapter 2: The Collapse Timeline

The Lie of Sudden Failure

Most people believe collapse happens all at once. One day you're functional, the next day you're not. This belief is comforting because it implies randomness—bad luck instead of inevitability. But collapse is rarely sudden. It is **cumulative**. What feels abrupt is usually the moment the final support gives way, not the moment the damage began.

Long before a breakdown is visible, the system has been compensating. You adjust sleep. You suppress emotion. You rationalize exhaustion. You normalize pain. Each adaptation buys time, but it also increases strain. Collapse is not a surprise attack—it is the receipt for unpaid costs.

The myth of sudden failure protects harmful systems. If collapse looks random, no one has to ask who benefited from your overextension. No one has to examine the structures that required you to sacrifice yourself to remain functional. The blame stays personal instead of systemic.

When you trace collapse backward, patterns emerge. The same stressors repeat. The same boundaries were crossed again and again. The same warnings were ignored. Collapse becomes legible once you stop focusing on the breaking point and start examining the **timeline**.

Understanding this timeline is not about regret. It is about accuracy. You cannot redesign what you refuse to map.

Phase One: Overextension

Collapse begins with giving more than you can sustainably give. Overextension often masquerades as virtue. Responsibility. Reliability. Strength. You become the one who handles it. The one who doesn't complain. The one who absorbs pressure so others don't have to.

In this phase, your capacity is slowly replaced by obligation. Rest becomes optional. Boundaries become negotiable. Your internal signals are overridden by external demands. You may still feel capable—but effort begins to cost more than it should.

Overextension is rewarded in the short term. Praise. Validation. Dependence. You are needed. That sense of being needed can feel stabilizing, even as it drains you. The system learns it can lean on you indefinitely.

The danger of overextension is that it feels like purpose. You confuse endurance with meaning. You mistake survival for success. By the time discomfort becomes obvious, the pattern is already entrenched.

This phase often lasts the longest. It is where collapse quietly incubates.

Phase Two: Signal Suppression

Eventually, the system starts sending warnings. Fatigue deepens. Motivation fluctuates. Emotional reactivity increases. Focus slips. These are not failures—they are **signals**. But signals are inconvenient. They slow output. They demand change.

So they are suppressed.

You push through exhaustion with discipline. You rationalize irritability. You numb anxiety. You tell yourself it's temporary. You minimize pain because acknowledging it would require renegotiation you feel you cannot afford.

Signal suppression is where self-betrayal becomes routine. You stop asking what you need and start asking what will keep things running. This is not because you are weak—it is because the cost of honesty feels too high.

The body and mind keep escalating signals when they are ignored. What begins as discomfort becomes dysfunction. What begins as fatigue becomes shutdown. Suppression works—until it doesn't.

This is where collapse becomes inevitable.

Phase Three: Identity Strain

When signals are suppressed long enough, identity begins to fracture. You can no longer sustain the version of yourself that made the system work. Roles feel heavy. Labels feel hollow. Motivation feels artificial.

This phase is often deeply confusing. You may still be functioning externally while internally unraveling. You may feel guilt for not being who you "used to be." You may attempt to double down, believing the problem is effort rather than architecture.

Identity strain is painful because identity once provided stability. It explained who you were and why you mattered. When it begins to fail, fear rushes in. Who are you if you stop performing? Who are you if you stop enduring?

This is often where shame peaks. You judge yourself for losing traits that were never meant to be permanent survival modes. You grieve versions of yourself that existed only because collapse hadn't happened yet.

Identity strain is not loss of self. It is loss of **false continuity**.

Phase Four: Functional Breakdown

Eventually, the system can no longer compensate. Performance drops. Memory falters. Emotions overwhelm or disappear. Tasks that were once automatic become impossible. This is the phase most people recognize as "the breakdown."

But by this point, collapse is already complete. What you are seeing is the aftermath, not the origin. The system has shut down non-essential functions to conserve resources. Survival takes priority over productivity.

This phase often triggers panic. Others may pressure you to recover quickly. You may pressure yourself even harder. The urge to return to baseline is strong, even though baseline was unsustainable.

Functional breakdown is often misdiagnosed as laziness, depression, or incompetence. In reality, it is **triage**. The system is protecting what remains by sacrificing what it can no longer support.

Nothing about this phase is moral. It is mechanical.

Phase Five: Forced Stillness

After collapse, stillness arrives—whether you choose it or not. Momentum dies. The future feels blank. Time stretches. This phase is often interpreted as stagnation, but it serves a critical purpose.

Stillness allows data to surface. Emotions previously suppressed emerge. Grief appears. Anger clarifies. Exhaustion deepens before it lifts. This is not regression—it is processing delayed costs.

The danger of forced stillness is rushing to escape it. When stillness is treated as failure, people attempt premature reintegration. They rebuild without redesign. They return to the same demands with fewer resources.

Stillness is where meaning can be rewritten. Not quickly. Not cleanly. But honestly. It is where you finally have access to information collapse made impossible to ignore.

If you skip this phase, collapse will repeat.

Phase Six: Timeline Awareness

The final phase is not recovery—it is **awareness**. You begin to see the entire arc. Not as a personal flaw, but as a predictable progression. You understand where you overextended, where you suppressed signals, where identity strained, where breakdown became inevitable.

This awareness is power. It removes mystery. It replaces shame with comprehension. You stop asking why you broke and start understanding why you survived as long as you did.

Timeline awareness allows you to intervene earlier next time. Not with more discipline, but with better structure. With boundaries. With redesign. With refusal.

This is where collapse stops being a threat and becomes a reference point.

You cannot unsee the timeline once you map it. And that is what makes rebuilding possible.

Exercises

Exercise 1: Personal Collapse Timeline
Purpose: Map your unique sequence of collapse.
Steps:

1. Draw a horizontal line across a page.
2. Mark when overextension began.
3. Add points for signal suppression, identity strain, and breakdown.
4. Write one sentence at each point describing what changed.
5. Circle the phase where intervention could have altered the outcome.

Exercise 2: Signal Inventory
Purpose: Identify warnings you were taught to ignore.
Steps:

1. List physical signals you dismissed.
2. List emotional signals you minimized.
3. List relational signals you rationalized.
4. Write what you told yourself at the time.
5. Rewrite each signal as information, not weakness.

Exercise 3: Identity Load Analysis
Purpose: Understand which identities carried unsustainable weight.
Steps:

1. List the roles you were performing before collapse.
2. Note what each role required you to suppress.
3. Identify which role collapsed first.
4. Write what that role protected you from.
5. Decide whether that role is meant to be rebuilt—or released.

Journal Prompts

1. When did I first feel something was wrong?
2. What did I normalize that should have alarmed me?
3. Which phase lasted the longest for me?
4. Where did I mistake endurance for strength?
5. What identity did collapse expose as unsustainable?
6. What support never arrived when I needed it?
7. What signals do I now recognize as intelligent?
8. How was stillness forced into my life?
9. What part of my timeline deserves compassion?
10. How does seeing the full arc change my self-blame?

Closing Reflection

Collapse does not arrive without warning—it arrives after warnings have been ignored, dismissed, or punished. When you see the timeline clearly, something shifts. Your story stops being about failure and starts being about survival under impossible conditions. This chapter is not about reliving pain. It is about reclaiming accuracy. Once you understand how collapse unfolded, you are no longer at its mercy. You gain the ability to design a future that does not require you to break in order to change.

Chapter 3: Becoming the Rubble Architect

From Victim to Designer

After collapse, most people are told to focus on recovery. Rest. Heal. Return. But recovery assumes a destination that already exists. It assumes you are meant to go back. Becoming the rubble architect begins when you realize there is **nothing to return to**—only something to build.

This shift is not denial of harm. It is not toxic positivity. It is agency reclaimed after damage. You are not pretending the collapse didn't happen; you are refusing to let it define you as passive debris. Rubble is not useless. Rubble is material.

Victimhood freezes time. It locks your identity to the moment of impact. While compassion for what you endured is essential, staying there indefinitely keeps the future unreachable. Architecture requires movement—measurement, choice, intention.

Becoming the rubble architect means accepting that you are standing in ruins **with tools**, not just wounds. You are the only one who can decide what is salvaged, what is discarded, and what is never rebuilt.

This chapter is about that moment of transition—when grief and clarity coexist, and responsibility returns without blame.

Claiming Authority in the Aftermath

Collapse strips authority away. Decisions were made for you—by circumstances, systems, bodies, limits. Even your own mind may have felt hijacked. The instinct afterward is to look outward for instructions. For permission. For rescue.

But architecture does not begin with consensus. It begins with **authority**—the authority to decide what matters now. This authority is quiet. It does not require confidence. It requires ownership.

Claiming authority does not mean you caused the collapse. It means you acknowledge that no one else can design what comes next. Waiting for external validation delays rebuilding. Waiting for certainty ensures stagnation.

Authority after collapse often feels fragile. You may doubt your judgment. You may fear repeating mistakes. That fear is understandable—but it is not a reason to abdicate responsibility. It is a reason to redesign more carefully.

Authority is not about control. It is about authorship.

Salvage Versus Sentiment

Not everything in the rubble deserves to be saved. This is where many people get stuck. Sentiment clings to structures that caused harm simply because they are familiar. Because they once worked. Because they are tied to identity.

Rubble architecture requires discernment. Salvage is intentional. It asks what still has structural integrity. What can be repurposed without reproducing the same stress fractures. What was valuable but misused.

Some skills survived collapse for a reason. Some values remain intact. Some relationships, though strained, hold truth. These are candidates for salvage. Others must be released, even if releasing them hurts.

Sentimentality rebuilds replicas. Discernment builds evolution. The difference is not cruelty—it is sustainability.

The goal is not to erase your past, but to **stop being loyal to what broke you**.

Designing Without Blueprints

One of the hardest parts of rebuilding is the absence of a clear plan. Blueprints belonged to the old system. They were based on assumptions that no longer apply. Trying to reuse them creates friction.

Rubble architects design iteratively. Small structures. Temporary supports. Experimental layouts. You test what holds. You adjust what collapses. You move slowly enough to listen to feedback.

This requires tolerance for uncertainty. You may not know who you are becoming. You may not recognize your priorities yet. That is not failure—it is early-stage construction.

Design without blueprints is not reckless. It is responsive. You build based on current capacity, not imagined potential. You allow the structure to evolve as you do.

This is how resilience becomes real—not aspirational.

Boundaries as Load-Bearing Walls

In the old structure, boundaries were optional or punished. You learned to compensate instead. In the new architecture, boundaries are non-negotiable. They are not preferences—they are **load-bearing walls**.

Without boundaries, everything collapses again. Energy leaks. Demands accumulate. Identity erodes. Boundaries define what the structure can hold without damage.

Rebuilding requires redefining your relationship to limits. Limits are not failures—they are design parameters. Ignoring them produces collapse. Honoring them produces longevity.

This may mean disappointing others. It may mean redefining roles. It may mean refusing access. None of these actions make you cruel. They make the structure viable.

Boundaries are not about keeping people out. They are about keeping the system intact.

Living in the Build Phase

Rebuilding does not happen all at once. You will live in the build phase longer than you expect. This phase is uncomfortable because it lacks polish. It feels incomplete. It invites judgment—from others and from yourself.

Living in the build phase requires patience and self-trust. You are not meant to have it all figured out. You are meant to stay responsive. To notice strain early. To adjust before fracture.

Progress in this phase is subtle. Increased clarity. Reduced resentment. Faster recovery after stress. These are signs the architecture is working.

Becoming the rubble architect means accepting that your life may never look "normal" again—but it can become **stable, honest, and sustainable**.

That is not a downgrade. It is a structural upgrade.

Exercises

Exercise 1: Salvage Inventory
Purpose: Identify what to keep, release, and redesign.
Steps:

1. List skills, values, and roles from before collapse.
2. Mark which ones caused strain.
3. Mark which ones supported you.
4. Decide whether each is salvageable, modifiable, or discardable.
5. Write one sentence explaining why.

Exercise 2: Authority Reclamation
Purpose: Reclaim decision-making power.
Steps:

1. Write three decisions you've been avoiding.
2. Identify what you're waiting for.
3. Remove the external factor.
4. Make a provisional decision.
5. Note how it feels to choose without permission.

Exercise 3: Boundary Blueprint
Purpose: Design protective limits.
Steps:

1. Identify where energy leaks occur.
2. Define one non-negotiable boundary.
3. Write how it will be enforced.
4. Anticipate resistance.
5. Write a response that does not over-explain.

Journal Prompts

1. What part of my identity collapsed that I secretly resented?
2. Where have I been waiting to be rescued?
3. What am I afraid to discard?
4. What still feels structurally sound within me?
5. How did lack of boundaries contribute to collapse?
6. What does authority feel like in my body?
7. What kind of life am I designing now?
8. What would sustainability look like daily?
9. Where am I rushing the rebuild?
10. What would it mean to trust my design process?

Closing Reflection

Becoming the rubble architect is not about control—it is about responsibility without blame. You did not choose the collapse, but you do choose what rises from it. This chapter is an invitation to step out of the debris and into authorship. You are not rebuilding to prove anything. You are rebuilding so the structure can hold you without breaking again.

Chapter 4: Fusion from Failure

Failure as Raw Material

Failure is usually treated as waste—something to hide, discard, or outgrow as quickly as possible. We are taught to minimize it, explain it away, or bury it under success stories. But failure is not debris. It is **raw material**. It contains information that success never provides.

Success tells you what worked under specific conditions. Failure tells you where the system failed to adapt. It reveals friction points, blind spots, and false assumptions. When something breaks, it exposes the architecture underneath. That exposure is invaluable—if you know how to read it.

Most people try to move past failure before they understand it. They rush toward reinvention without integration. The result is a brittle version of growth—strong on the surface, fragile underneath. Fusion from failure requires staying with the data long enough to extract meaning.

Failure hurts because it contradicts identity. It challenges the story you were told about who you are supposed to be. That pain tempts avoidance. But avoidance turns failure into a repeating pattern instead of a learning event.

This chapter is about transforming failure from something that defines you into something that **builds you**—not by erasing it, but by integrating it.

Why Integration Matters More Than Recovery

Recovery aims to restore function. Integration aims to evolve function. Recovery asks, "How do I get back to where I was?" Integration asks, "What does this failure need to become part of?"

When failure is not integrated, it remains external—something that happened *to* you rather than something that changed you. Unintegrated failure resurfaces as fear, avoidance, overcompensation, or perfectionism. It silently shapes behavior while remaining unacknowledged.

Integration allows failure to become internalized wisdom instead of external threat. You stop reacting to it and start using it. The nervous system relaxes when it understands the lesson has been learned.

This is why people who "bounce back" quickly often break again. The failure was bypassed, not fused. The system resets without upgrading. Old vulnerabilities remain.

Fusion is slower than recovery—but it is permanent.

The Mechanics of Fusion

Fusion is not acceptance alone. It is **structural incorporation**. Like alloying metals, fusion changes the properties of the whole. The weakness that once caused fracture becomes a source of flexibility, precision, or restraint.

To fuse failure, you must identify what failed, why it failed, and what capacity was missing at the time. Capacity is key. Failure often occurs not because of lack of effort, but because the system lacked boundaries, resources, or adaptability.

Once identified, failure becomes a design input. You do not ask how to avoid it next time—you ask how to design a system that can survive it. This shifts your relationship to risk. Fear is replaced with preparedness.

Fusion also dissolves shame. Shame thrives on isolation. When failure is fused into identity, it loses its power to exile you from yourself.

You are no longer trying to outrun your past—you are carrying it forward in a different form.

From Scar to Structure

Scars are often seen as evidence of damage. In reality, scars are evidence of survival. They mark where reinforcement occurred. But scars alone are passive—they show where healing happened, not how strength was gained.

Fusion turns scars into **structure**. Instead of merely remembering what hurt, you redesign behavior, boundaries, and expectations around what you learned. The lesson becomes active.

This is where people often resist. Structure requires commitment. It requires saying no. It requires changing how you operate, not just how you think. Many would rather keep the scar than change the system that caused it.

But structure is what prevents recurrence. It is how experience becomes protection instead of trauma. It is how pain becomes leverage.

When scars become structure, you stop reliving failure and start benefiting from it.

Reclaiming Agency Through Synthesis

Failure often strips agency. It makes you doubt your judgment. You question whether you can trust yourself again. Fusion restores agency by reframing failure as **participation in learning**, not proof of incompetence.

You begin to see where you had limited information. Where you acted reasonably under flawed assumptions. Where the system was rigged against sustainability. This clarity replaces self-blame with responsibility.

Agency does not mean control over outcomes. It means influence over design. You cannot prevent all failure—but you can decide how it shapes you.

Synthesis is where agency returns. You are no longer defined by what went wrong. You are defined by how you integrated it.

This is the difference between being shaped by failure and being forged by it.

Living as an Alloy, Not a Fix

Once fusion occurs, you do not return to a "pure" version of yourself. You become an alloy—stronger in some ways, more flexible in others, less brittle overall. You carry the memory of failure without being ruled by it.

Living as an alloy means accepting complexity. You may be cautious and courageous. Tender and firm. Slower and more precise. These are not contradictions—they are results of integration.

You stop chasing invulnerability. You stop needing to prove resilience. You trust the structure because it has been tested.

Fusion does not make you flawless. It makes you **durable**.

That is the upgrade failure offers—if you allow it to fuse.

Exercises

Exercise 1: Failure Deconstruction

Purpose: Extract usable information from a past failure.
Steps:

1. Choose one failure that still carries emotional weight.
2. Describe what happened without judgment.
3. Identify what assumptions were present.
4. Note what capacity was missing at the time.
5. Write one structural change that would alter the outcome now.

Exercise 2: Scar-to-Structure Translation
Purpose: Convert pain into design.
Steps:

1. Identify an emotional scar you still react to.
2. Write what it taught you.
3. Identify one boundary it demands.
4. Identify one behavior it requires you to change.
5. Write how this becomes protection rather than avoidance.

Exercise 3: Alloy Identity Mapping
Purpose: Redefine self after fusion.
Steps:

1. List traits you had before failure.
2. List traits gained after failure.
3. Identify where tension exists between them.
4. Write how both can coexist.
5. Describe the person you are becoming as a synthesis.

Journal Prompts

1. What failure still feels unresolved?
2. What did that failure teach me about my limits?
3. Where have I been trying to erase instead of integrate?
4. How has shame kept failure from becoming wisdom?
5. What structural changes have I avoided making?
6. What capacity do I now have that I didn't before?
7. How does my relationship to risk need to change?
8. What would durability look like in my life?
9. Where am I stronger because I broke?
10. What does fusion feel like emotionally?

Closing Reflection

Failure does not diminish you unless it remains unfused. When you integrate what broke, you stop carrying it as a threat and start carrying it as strength. This chapter is not about reframing failure as success—it is about transforming it into structure. You are not meant to be restored to who you were before. You are meant to become something that could not exist without what failed.

Chapter 5: Victory Through Implosion

Why Collapse Can Be a Win

Victory is usually imagined as expansion—more power, more momentum, more visibility. Implosion looks like the opposite. Energy turns inward. Structures compress. Movement slows or stops entirely. From the outside, implosion looks like defeat.

But implosion is not collapse outward. It is **collapse inward with containment**. Nothing spills. Nothing scatters. The energy that once leaked into unsustainable structures is pulled back into the core.

In physics, implosion increases density. Pressure builds inward, not outward. The result is not disappearance—it is concentration. The same principle applies to human systems. When you stop performing, explaining, proving, and overextending, power returns to where it belongs.

Implosion feels terrifying because it removes external validation. You are no longer expanding into others' expectations. You are compressing into your own truth. That compression is uncomfortable—but it is not empty.

Victory through implosion means you stop losing energy to structures that cannot sustain you. What looks like retreat is actually **reclamation**.

The End of Leaking Power

Before implosion, power leaks constantly. It leaks through people-pleasing. Through over-functioning. Through emotional labor that is never reciprocated. Through identities that require constant maintenance.

Leaking power feels normal when it has always been demanded. You may not even recognize it as loss—only as fatigue, resentment, or numbness. Implosion begins when the system refuses to leak any further.

This refusal often appears as withdrawal. Silence. Reduced output. Decreased tolerance for noise. These changes are frequently misinterpreted as depression or disengagement. In reality, they are **containment responses**.

By pulling energy inward, the system creates the conditions for regeneration. You stop funding what drains you. You stop feeding roles that hollow you out. Power returns to the center because it is no longer being siphoned away.

Containment is not isolation. It is conservation.

Silence as Strategic Compression

Silence is one of the first signs of implosion. Not awkward silence—but deliberate quiet. Fewer explanations. Less emotional broadcasting. Reduced need to be understood.

This silence is not emptiness. It is **pressure building**. When you stop narrating yourself to others, you regain access to your internal signal. Thoughts sharpen. Priorities clarify. Boundaries become easier to feel.

People often rush to fill silence because silence disrupts access. When you go quiet, others lose leverage. They can no longer predict you, manage you, or extract reassurance. This makes silence uncomfortable for those accustomed to your availability.

But silence is not punishment. It is recalibration. It allows your system to compress around what matters rather than expanding to accommodate everything else.

Silence is not withdrawal from life. It is withdrawal from unnecessary expenditure.

Shrinking to Strengthen

Implosion reduces scale. Your world may get smaller. Fewer commitments. Fewer people. Fewer goals. This shrinking is often misread as loss—but scale reduction increases **structural integrity**.

Large systems fail when they exceed their capacity to self-regulate. Smaller systems are easier to stabilize. When you shrink intentionally, you regain control over variables that once overwhelmed you.

This may require grieving what you can no longer sustain. Certain ambitions. Certain relationships. Certain identities. Grief does not mean you chose wrong—it means the cost became visible.

Shrinking does not mean you are becoming less. It means you are becoming **accurate**. You are aligning scale with capacity instead of fantasy.

Strength built at the right scale lasts.

Internal Alignment Over External Momentum

External momentum is seductive. It feels like progress. But momentum without alignment leads straight back to fracture. Implosion interrupts momentum so alignment can occur.

When energy is inward-facing, you begin to notice misalignments that were invisible during expansion. Values clarify. Limits assert themselves. Desire becomes distinguishable from obligation.

This alignment phase can feel stagnant because movement is internal. But internal realignment determines whether future expansion will be sustainable or destructive.

Victory here is subtle. It is choosing coherence over speed. Integrity over approval. Stability over spectacle.

This is where true power consolidates.

When Implosion Becomes Sovereignty

The final stage of implosion is sovereignty. Not domination. Not control. **Self-governance**. You decide where energy goes. You decide what structures are fed.

Sovereignty emerges when you stop needing collapse to enforce limits. You no longer require breakdown to say no. Implosion teaches restraint before catastrophe.

At this stage, you may still move slowly—but every movement is intentional. Expansion, when it comes, is deliberate rather than compulsive.

Victory through implosion is not loud. It is not celebrated publicly. But it is unmistakable internally.

You are no longer leaking. You are no longer fracturing. You are no longer surviving by expansion.

You are operating from the core.

Exercises

Exercise 1: Power Leak Identification
Purpose: Identify where energy is being lost.
Steps:

1. List situations that leave you drained.
2. Identify what you give in those situations.
3. Note whether it is reciprocated.
4. Decide whether the exchange is sustainable.
5. Write one action to stop the leak.

Exercise 2: Strategic Shrink
Purpose: Reduce scale to regain strength.
Steps:

1. List all current commitments.
2. Mark which are essential.
3. Mark which are optional.
4. Choose one optional commitment to pause or end.
5. Note the internal response to shrinking.

Exercise 3: Silence Practice
Purpose: Build containment through reduced output.
Steps:

1. Choose one area where you over-explain.
2. Commit to fewer words for one week.
3. Observe internal reactions.
4. Observe others' reactions.
5. Write what clarity emerges.

Journal Prompts

1. Where has my energy been leaking?
2. What feels threatening about shrinking?
3. How do I react to silence?
4. What do I gain by staying loud?
5. Where do I confuse expansion with progress?
6. What boundaries require no explanation?
7. What scale feels sustainable now?
8. How does containment feel in my body?
9. What would sovereignty look like daily?
10. What kind of victory do I no longer want?

Closing Reflection

Implosion is not the opposite of victory—it is its prerequisite. By pulling inward, you reclaim what was scattered, wasted, or extracted. This chapter marks the shift from survival through expansion to strength through containment. Victory through implosion is quiet, disciplined, and deeply personal. But once power is centralized, it cannot be taken the same way again.

Appendix A: The Breakdown Recovery Meditation

This meditation is designed for moments when your system feels fractured, overloaded, or hollowed out—when thinking harder no longer helps and forcing forward only deepens exhaustion. It is not a visualization meant to escape reality, nor a relaxation exercise meant to override discomfort. This is a **recovery protocol**: a way to stabilize, re-center, and gently reassemble capacity after breakdown.

You can return to this meditation repeatedly. Each time, it will meet you where you are—not where you think you should be.

Preparation: Setting the Conditions

Choose a position that requires **no effort to maintain**. Sitting, lying down, or leaning is fine. The goal is structural support, not posture perfection. If your body needs to shift during the meditation, allow it.

Silence is helpful but not required. If noise exists, treat it as background data rather than interruption. This practice is about integration, not control.

Close your eyes if that feels safe. If not, soften your gaze and let your vision blur.

Before beginning, say silently—or out loud if you prefer:

"I am not here to fix myself. I am here to recover capacity."

Let that sentence settle without forcing belief.

Phase One: Grounding the Fractured System

Bring attention to your breath without changing it. Notice where breathing is easiest to feel—nose, chest, belly, or throat. There is no correct location.

For the next several breaths, simply **track the inhale and exhale** like data points. Inhale: something enters. Exhale: something leaves. Nothing else is required.

If thoughts arise, do not push them away. Imagine placing them gently beside you, like tools set down temporarily. You are not discarding them—just pausing their use.

Now bring awareness to the weight of your body. Notice where gravity holds you. Let yourself be held. You do not need to hold yourself together right now.

If your system feels scattered, name it silently: *scattered*. If it feels numb, name it: *numb*. Naming is grounding. It turns chaos into information.

Stay here for several breaths, letting your system register that **no action is required**.

Phase Two: Locating the Point of Overload

Gently scan your body from head to feet. You are not searching for pain—you are noticing **density**. Where does your system feel heaviest, tightest, or most compressed?

When you find a place that draws attention, rest there. Do not analyze it. Just notice it exists.

Now imagine that this area represents **accumulated load**—everything you carried past capacity. Expectations. Pressure. Survival. Endurance.

On each inhale, imagine space forming around this area. Not removing the load—just creating room for it to exist without crushing you.

On each exhale, imagine pressure softening slightly. Even a 1% reduction is enough. Recovery is incremental.

If emotion arises here, allow it. Emotion is energy moving through structure. You do not need to interpret it.

Remain with this area until the intensity stabilizes or shifts, however subtly.

Phase Three: Separating Identity from Collapse

Bring attention to the idea of *who you were* during the breakdown. Not to judge—only to observe.

Now say silently:

"That version of me was operating beyond sustainable limits."

Let the sentence land without argument.

Imagine that version of you standing a few steps away—not abandoned, not rejected, just **distinct**. You can see them clearly without being inside them.

Notice what they were trying to protect. What they were trying to maintain. Acknowledge the effort without romanticizing the cost.

Now imagine turning slightly toward your current self—the one breathing here, supported, present. This is not a better self. It is a **different operational state**.

Say silently:

"I am allowed to evolve past survival."

Let the distance between identities create relief rather than loss.

Phase Four: Reclaiming Central Authority

Bring awareness to the center of your chest or abdomen—wherever feels like a natural core.

Imagine this area as a **control center**, not rigid or dominating, but steady. A place where decisions are made slowly and intentionally.

With each inhale, imagine energy returning here—from places it has been leaking. From overthinking. From people-pleasing. From vigilance.

You do not need to retrieve energy consciously. Simply allow it to return when it is ready.

With each exhale, imagine this center becoming clearer, quieter, more defined.

Now say silently:

"I decide what my system carries."

You do not need to know what that means yet. Authority can exist before clarity.

Rest here for several breaths, letting containment rebuild.

Phase Five: Gentle Reintegration

Now imagine your internal system as a structure that has survived damage but remains standing. Some areas reinforced. Some under reconstruction. None condemned.

Visualize fragments—not as broken pieces, but as **specialized components** returning to alignment. Fatigue finding rest. Anger finding boundaries. Grief finding space.

You are not forcing coherence. You are allowing proximity.

Say silently:

"Everything that belongs can return at its own pace."

If resistance appears, acknowledge it. Resistance is often a protector. Thank it for its vigilance without negotiating further.

Notice how your breath moves now. Notice any shift in temperature, pressure, or tone. These are signs of integration.

Phase Six: Closing the Meditation

Begin to deepen your breath slightly. Feel the boundary of your body again—the edges, the weight, the contact with support.

If your eyes are closed, imagine light entering gradually rather than suddenly.

Before ending, say silently:

"Recovery is happening, even when I cannot feel it."

This is not affirmation—it is recognition of process.

When you are ready, open your eyes or refocus your gaze. Move slowly. Recovery respects transitions.

Aftercare and Use Notes

- This meditation can be used **daily**, or during moments of overwhelm, shutdown, or post-exertion.
- If emotions linger afterward, allow time before returning to tasks. Integration continues after the practice ends.
- You do not need to feel "better" for the meditation to work. Reduced strain, increased clarity, or slower reactivity are valid outcomes.
- If intense distress or dissociation persists, consider additional support. This meditation is a stabilizer, not a substitute for care.

Closing Reflection

Breakdown recovery is not about rebuilding who you were. It is about restoring capacity so something truer can emerge. This meditation does not demand insight, belief, or effort—only presence. Each time you return to it, you teach your system that collapse does not mean abandonment. It means recalibration. And recalibration, done gently, becomes resilience over time.

Message from the Author:

I hope you enjoyed this book, I love astrology and knew there was not a book such as this out on the shelf. I love metaphysical items as well. Please check out my other books:

-Life of Government Benefits

-My life of Hell

-My life with Hydrocephalus

-Red Sky

-World Domination:Woman's rule

-World Domination:Woman's Rule 2: The War

-Life and Banishment of Apophis: book 1

-The Kidney Friendly Diet

-The Ultimate Hemp Cookbook

-Creating a Dispensary(legally)

-Cleanliness throughout life: the importance of showering from childhood to adulthood.

-Strong Roots: The Risks of Overcoddling children

-Hemp Horoscopes: Cosmic Insights and Earthly Healing

- Celestial Hemp Navigating the Zodiac: Through the Green Cosmos

-Astrological Hemp: Aligning The Stars with Earth's Ancient Herb

-The Astrological Guide to Hemp: Stars, Signs, and Sacred Leaves

-Green Growth: Innovative Marketing Strategies for your Hemp Products and Dispensary

-Cosmic Cannabis

-Astrological Munchies

-Henry The Hemp

-Zodiacal Roots: The Astrological Soul Of Hemp

- Green Constellations: Intersection of Hemp and Zodiac

-Hemp in The Houses: An astrological Adventure Through The Cannabis Galaxy

-Galactic Ganja Guide

Heavenly Hemp

Zodiac Leaves

Doctor Who Astrology

Cannastrology

Stellar Satvias and Cosmic Indicas

Celestial Cannabis: A Zodiac Journey

AstroHerbology: The Sky and The Soil: Volume 1

AstroHerbology:Celestial Cannabis:Volume 2

Cosmic Cannabis Cultivation

The Starry Guide to Herbal Harmony: Volume 1

The Starry Guide to Herbal Harmony: Cannabis Universe: Volume 2

Yugioh Astrology: Astrological Guide to Deck, Duels and more

Nightmare Mansion: Echoes of The Abyss

Nightmare Mansion 2: Legacy of Shadows

Nightmare Mansion 3: Shadows of the Forgotten

Nightmare Mansion 4: Echoes of the Damned

The Life and Banishment of Apophis: Book 2

Nightmare Mansion: Halls of Despair

Healing with Herb: Cannabis and Hydrocephalus

Planetary Pot: Aligning with Astrological Herbs: Volume 1

Fast Track to Freedom: 30 Days to Financial Independence Using AI, Assets, and Agile Hustles

Cosmic Hemp Pathways

How to Become Financially Free in 30 Days: 10,000 Paths to Prosperity

Zodiacal Herbage: Astrological Insights: Volume 1

Nightmare Mansion: Whispers in the Walls

The Daleks Invade Atlantis

Henry the hemp and Hydrocephalus

10X The Kidney Friendly Diet

Cannabis Universe: Adult coloring book

Hemp Astrology: The Healing Power of the Stars

Zodiacal Herbage: Astrological Insights: Cannabis Universe: Volume 2

Planetary Pot: Aligning with Astrological Herbs: Cannabis Universes: Volume 2

Doctor Who: Convergence Protocol – The Replicator War

Nightmare Mansion: Curse of the Blood Moon

The Celestial Stoner: A Guide to the Zodiac

Cosmic Pleasures: Sex Toy Astrology for Every Sign

Hydrocephalus Astrology: Navigating the Stars and Healing Waters

Lapis and the Mischievous Chocolate Bar

Celestial Positions: Sexual Astrology for Every Sign

Apophis's Shadow Work Journal: **:** A Journey of Self-Discovery and Healing

Kinky Cosmos: Sexual Kink Astrology for Every Sign

Digital Cosmos: The Astrological Digimon Compendium

Stellar Seeds: The Cosmic Guide to Growing with Astrology

Apophis's Daily Gratitude Journal

Cat Astrology: Feline Mysteries of the Cosmos

The Cosmic Kama Sutra: An Astrological Guide to Sexual Positions

Unleash Your Potential: A Guided Journal Powered by AI Insights

Whispers of the Enchanted Grove

Cosmic Pleasures: An Astrological Guide to Sexual Kinks

369, 12 Manifestation Journal

Whisper of the nocturne journal(blank journal for writing or drawing)

The Boogey Book

Locked In Reflection: A Chastity Journey Through Locktober

Generating Wealth Quickly:How to Generate $100,000 in 24 Hours

Star Magic: Harness the Power of the Universe

The Flatulence Chronicles: A Fart Journal for Self-Discovery

The Doctor and The Death Moth

Seize the Day: A Personal Seizure Tracking Journal

The Ultimate Boogeyman Safari: A Journey into the Boogie World and Beyond

Whispers of Samhain: 1,000 Spells of Love, Luck, and Lunar Magic: Samhain Spell Book

Apophis's guides:Witch's Spellbook Crafting Guide for Halloween

Frost & Flame: The Enchanted Yule Grimoire of 1000 Winter Spells

The Ultimate Boogey Goo Guide & Spooky Activities for Halloween Fun

Harmony of the Scales: A Libra's Spellcraft for Balance and Beauty

The Enchanted Advent: 36 Days of Christmas Wonders

Nightmare Mansion: The Labyrinth of Screams

Harvest of Enchantment: 1,000 Spells of Gratitude, Love, and Fortune for Thanksgiving

The Boogey Chronicles: A Journal of Nightly Encounters and Shadowy Secrets

The 12 Days of Financial Freedom: A Step-by-Step Christmas Countdown to Transform Your Finances

Sigil of the Eternal Spiral Blank Journal

A Christmas Feast: Timeless Recipes for Every Meal

Holiday Stress-Free Solutions: A Survival Guide to Thriving During the Festive Season

Yu-Gi-Oh! Holiday Gifting Mastery: The Ultimate Guide for Fans and Newcomers Alike

Holiday Harmony: A Hydrocephalus Survival Guide for the Festive Season

Celestial Craft: The Witch's Almanac for 2025 – A Cosmic Guide to Manifestations, Moons, and Mystical Events

Doctor Who: The Toymaker's Winter Wonderland

Tulsa King Unveiled: A Thrilling Guide to Stallone's Mafia Masterpiece

Pendulum Craft: A Complete Guide to Crafting and Using Personalized Divination Tools

Nightmare Mansion: Santa's Eternal Eve

Starlight Noel: A Cosmic Journey through Christmas Mysteries

The Dark Architect: Unlocking the Blueprint of Existence

Surviving the Embrace: The Ultimate Guide to Encounters with The Hugging Molly

The Enchanted Codex: Secrets of the Craft for Witches, Wiccans, and Pagans

Harvest of Gratitude: A Complete Thanksgiving Guide

Yuletide Essentials: A Complete Guide to an Authentic and Magical Christmas

Celestial Smokes: A Cosmic Guide to Cigars and Astrology

Living in Balance: A Comprehensive Survival Guide to Thriving with Diabetes Insipidus

Cosmic Symbiosis: The Venom Zodiac Chronicles

The Cursed Paw of Ambition

Cosmic Symbiosis: The Astrological Venom Journal

Celestial Wonders Unfold: A Stargazer's Guide to the Cosmos (2024-2029)

The Ultimate Black Friday Prepper's Guide: Mastering Shopping Strategies and Savings

Cosmic Sales: The Astrological Guide to Black Friday Shopping

Legends of the Corn Mother and Other Harvest Myths

Whispers of the Harvest: The Corn Mother's Journal

The Evergreen Spellbook

The Doctor Meets the Boogeyman

The White Witch of Rose Hall's SpellBook

The Gingerbread Golem's Shadow: A Study in Sweet Darkness

The Gingerbread Golem Codex: An Academic Exploration of Sweet Myths

The Gingerbread Golem Grimoire: Sweet Magicks and Spells for the Festive Witch

The Curse of the Gingerbread Golem

10-minute Christmas Crafts for kids

Christmas Crisis Solutions: The Ultimate Last-Minute Survival Guide

Gingerbread Golem Recipes: Holiday Treats with a Magical Twist

The Infinite Key: Unlocking Mystical Secrets of the Ages

Enchanted Yule: A Wiccan and Pagan Guide to a Magical and Memorable Season

Dinosaurs of Power: Unlocking Ancient Magick

Astro-Dinos: The Cosmic Guide to Prehistoric Wisdom

Gallifrey's Yule Logs: A Festive Doctor Who Cookbook

The Dino Grimoire: Secrets of Prehistoric Magick

The Gift They Never Knew They Needed

The Gingerbread Golem's Culinary Alchemy: Enchanting Recipes for a Sweetly Dark Feast

A Time Lord Christmas: Holiday Adventures with the Doctor

Krampusproofing Your Home: Defensive Strategies for Yule

Silent Frights: A Collection of Christmas Creepypastas to Chill Your Bones

Santa Raptor's Jolly Carnage: A Dino-Claus Christmas Tale

Prehistoric Palettes: A Dino Wicca Coloring Journey

The Christmas Wishkeeper Chronicles

The Starlight Sleigh: A Holiday Journey

Elf Secrets: The True Magic of the North Pole

Candy Cane Conjurations

Cooking with Kids: Recipes Under 20 Minutes

Doctor Who: The TARDIS Confiscation

The Anxiety First Aid Kit: Quick Tools to Calm Your Mind

Frosty Whispers: A Winter's Tale

The Infinite Key: Unlocking the Secrets to Prosperity, Resilience, and Purpose

The Grasping Void: Why You'll Regret This Purchase

Astrology for Busy Bees: Star Signs Simplified

The Instant Focus Formula: Cut Through the Noise

The Secret Language of Colors: Unlocking the Emotional Codes

Sacred Fossil Chronicles: Blank Journal

The Christmas Cottage Miracle

Feeding Frenzy: Graboid-Inspired Recipes

Manifest in Minutes: The Quick Law of Attraction Guide

The Symbiote Chronicles: Doctor Who's Venomous Journey

Think Tiny, Grow Big: The Minimalist Mindset

The Energy Key: Unlocking Limitless Motivation

New Year, New Magic: Manifesting Your Best Year Yet

Unstoppable You: Mastering Confidence in Minutes

Infinite Energy: The Secret to Never Feeling Drained

Lightning Focus: Mastering the Art of Productivity in a Distracted World

Saturnalia Manifestation Magick: A Guide to Unlocking Abundance During the Solstice

Graboids and Garland: The Ultimate Tremors-Themed Christmas Guide

12 Nights of Holiday Magic

The Power of Pause: 60-Second Mindfulness Practices

The Quick Reset: How to Reclaim Your Life After Burnout
The Shadow Eater: A Tale of Despair and Survival
The Micro-Mastery Method: Transform Your Skills in Just Minutes a Day
Reclaiming Time: How to Live More by Doing Less
Chronovore: The Eternal Nexus
The Mind Reset: Unlocking Your Inner Peace in a Chaotic World
Confidence Code: Building Unshakable Self-Belief
Baby the Vampire Terrier
Baby the Vampire Terrier's Christmas Adventure
Celestial Streams: The Content Creator's Astrology Manual
The Wealth Whisperer: Unlocking Abundance with Everyday Actions
The Energy Equation: Maximize Your Output Without Burning Out
The Happiness Algorithm: Science-Backed Steps to Joyful Living
Stress-Free Success: Achieving Goals Without Anxiety
Mindful Wealth: The New Blueprint for Financial Freedom
The Festive Flavors of New Year: A Culinary Celebration
The Master's Gambit: Keys of Eternal Power
Shadowed Secrets: Groundhog Day Mysteries
Beneath the Burrow: Lessons from the Groundhog
Spring's Whispers: The Groundhog's Prediction
The Limitless Mindset: Unlock Your Untapped Potential
The Focus Funnel: How to Cut Through Chaos and Get Results
Bold Moves: Building Courage to Live on Your Terms
The Daily Shift: Simple Practices for Lasting Transformation
The Quarter-Life Reset: Thriving in Your 20s and 30s
The Art of Shadowplay: Building Your Own Personal Myth
The Eternal Loop: Finding Purpose in Repetition
Burrowing Wisdom: Life Lessons from the Groundhog
Shadow Work: A Groundhog Day Perspective
Love in Bloom: 5-Minute Romantic Gestures

The Shadowspell Codex: Secrets of Forbidden Magick
The Burnout Cure: Finding Balance in a Busy World
The Groundhog Prophecy: Unlocking Seasonal Secrets
Nog Tales: The Spirited History of Eggnog
Six More Weeks: Embracing Seasonal Transitions
The Lumivian Chronicles: Fragments of the Fifth Dimension
Money on Your Mind: A Beginner's Guide to Wealth
The Focus Fix: Breaking Through Distraction
January's Spirit Keepers: Mystical Protectors of the Cold
Creativity Unchained: Unlocking Your Wildest Ideas in 2025
Manifestation Mastery: 365 Days to Rewrite Your Reality
The Groundhog's Mirror: Reflecting on Change
The Weeping Angels' Christmas Curse
Burrowed in Time: A Groundhog Day Journey
Heartbeats: Poems to Share with Your Valentine
Dino Wicca: The Sacred Grimoire of Prehistoric Magick
Courage of the Pride: Finding Your Inner Roar
The Lion's Leap: Bold Moves for Big Results
Healthy Hustle: Achieving Without Overworking
Practical Manifesting: Turning Dreams into Reality in 2025
Jurassic Pharaohs: Unlocking the Magick of Ancient Egypt and Dino Wicca
The Happiness Equation: Small Changes for Big Joy
The Confidence Compass: Finding Your Inner Strength
Whispers in the Hollow: Tales of the Forgotten Beasts
Echoes from the Hollow: The Return of Forgotten Beasts
The Hollow Ascendant: The Rise of the Forgotten Beasts
The Relationship Reset: Building Better Connections
Mastering the Morning: How to Win the Day Before 8 AM
The Shadow's Dance: Groundhog Day Symbolism
Cupid's Kitchen: Quick Valentine's Day Recipes
Valentine's Day on a Budget: Love Without Breaking the Bank
Astrocraft: Aligning the Stars in the World of Minecraft

Forecasting Life: Groundhog Day Reflections

Bleeding Hearts: Twisted Tales of Valentine's Terror

Herbal Smoke Revolution: The Ultimate Guide to Nature's Cigarette Alternative

Winter's Wrath: The Complete Survival Blueprint for Extreme Freezes.

The Groundhog's Shadow: A Tale of Seasons

Burrowed Insights: Wisdom from the Groundhog

Sensual Strings: The Art of Erotic Bondage

Whispered Flames: Unlocking the Power of Fire Play

Forgotten Shadows: A Guide to Cryptids Lost to Time

Six Weeks of Secrets: Groundhog Day's Hidden Messages

Shadows and Cycles: Groundhog Day Reflections

The Art of Love Letters: Crafting the Perfect Message

Romantic Getaways at Home: Turning Your Space into Paradise

Purrfect Brews: A Cat Lover's Guide to Coffee and Companionship

The Groundhog's Wisdom: Timeless Lessons for Modern Life

The Shadow Oracle: Groundhog Day as a Predictor

Emerging from the Burrow: A Journey of Renewal

The Language of Love: Learning Your Partner's Love Style

Authorpreneur: The Ultimate Blueprint for Writing, Publishing, and Thriving as an Author

Weathering the Seasons: Groundhog Day Perspectives

Valentine's Day Magic: A Guide to Romantic Rituals

The Shadow Chronicles: Stories of Groundhog Day

Love and Laughter: Fun Games for Valentine's Day

AstroRealty: Unlocking the Stars for Property Success

The Groundhog's Path: A Guide to Seasonal Balance

Groundhog Day Diaries: Reflections in the Shadow

The Groundhog's Light: Illuminating the Path Ahead

Valentine's Traditions from Around the World

AI Wealth Revolution: Unlocking the Trillionaire Mindset
Love Rekindled: Reigniting Passion in Relationships
Single and Thriving: Self-Love on Valentine's Day
Emerald Legends: Mystical Tales of Ireland
Green Alchemy: Harnessing Nature's Magic
The Hearts of Horror: A Valentine's Day Nightmare
The Leprechaun's Guide to Wealth and Wisdom
Dancing with the Sidhe: Celebrating the Otherworld
Shamrocks and Shadows: Mysteries of the Green Isle
Emerald Energy: Harnessing Luck and Growth
The Gingerbread Golem's Valentine: A Sweetheart's Guide to Love and Enchantment
The Celtic Knot: Weaving Life and Destiny
Green Fire: Elemental Magic for St. Patrick's Day
Clover Chronicles: Finding Your Inner Luck
Ireland's Mystical Creatures: A Field Guide
Gingerbread Golem's Love Almanac
Prowl and Thrive: The Lion's Guide to Success
Love Alchemy: Transforming Your Life Through Heart Energy
WORLD DOMINATION: Woman's Rule 3:The New Life
The Midnight Rose: A Guide to Lunar Love Spells
The Forbidden Letters: Writing Your Own Love Prophecy
Luck and Lore: St. Patrick's Day for Modern Mystics
The Green Path: A Pagan Celebration of Renewal
The Dark Architect's Guide to Reprogramming Reality
Prankster's Paradise: A Guide to Harmless Hijinks
Manifest Your Reality: The Law of Attraction Simplified
The TARDIS Owner's Manual: Understanding the Doctor's Ship: *A complete guide to the TARDIS, its technology, secrets, and mysteries*
Starlit Romance: Astrology Secrets for Finding True Love

The Time Lord's Atlas: A Complete Guide to the Whoniverse: *A breakdown of the locations, planets, and dimensions explored in Doctor Who*

Sweetheart Shadows: The Dark Side of Love and Attraction

February Fire: Reigniting Passion in Every Area of Life

The Self-Love Toolkit: 5 Ways to Embrace Who You Are

February Sparks: Ignite Your Dreams in 28 Days

March to Success: A 31-Day Action Blueprint

Ancient Paths: The 13 Sacred Principles of Dino Wicca

Echoes of Tomorrow: Navigating the AI Revolution

The Wellness Blueprint: Balancing Mind, Body, and Soul

Green Horizons: Sustainable Living for a Better Tomorrow

The AI Wealth Code: How to Make Millions with Automation

AI-Powered Creativity: Writing, Art, and Music for Profit

Extinction Rites: Rebirthing Your Soul Through Prehistoric Magick

Sacred Serpents tarot

Celestial Enchantment blank journal

Star Strains

Culinary Journeys: Exploring Global Flavors at Home

The Hollowvale Curse

The Hollowvale Harvest

The Egg of Transformation: Awakening Your Inner Power

Blooming Into Power: A Wiccan Guide to Spring Awakening

The Nightmare Nexus: The Third Doctor's Perilous Haunting

Digital Detox: Reclaiming Your Life in a Connected World

Ostara's Path: Walking the Spiral of Renewal

The Sacred Hare

Financial Freedom: Building Wealth in the Modern Age

Spring's Cauldron: Stirring the Waters of Change

The Hollowvale Pact

Quantum Consciousness: The Science of Reality Shifting

The Hollowvale Hunger

The Sacred Waters Within: A Witch's Guide to Hydrocephalus Magick

The Raven's Nest: Building a Life of Unshakable Stability

AI and the Human Mind: The Future of Intelligence

The Hollowvale Reckoning

Timeless Love: Building and Maintaining Lasting Relationships

The Raven's Roar: Unlocking Unstoppable Confidence

Raven Sight: Awakening Intuition and Inner Wisdom

The Butterfly Effect: Small Changes, Big Transformations

Taming the Boogeyman: How to Conquer Your Inner Fears

The Magick of Green: Awakening Earth's Energy in You

The Entrepreneurial Mindset: Secrets to Business Success

The Hollowvale End

The Shadow Luck Ritual: Reclaiming Power from Your Dark Side

Spring Magick for Beginners: A Simple Guide to Seasonal Energy Work

Doctor Who: The Hollowvale Conundrum

The March of Miracles: Unlocking Synchronicities in Spring

Unveiling the Cosmos: A Guide to Stargazing and Space Exploration

The Ultimate Guide to Surviving an Economic Collapse

The AI Gold Rush: How to Profit from the AI Revolution

Bastet's Shadow: The Hidden Power of Feline Magick

The Bastet Codex: Unlocking the Goddess's Magickal Secrets

Purring Spells: Harnessing Bastet's Healing Frequencies

Bastet's Nine Lives: Rebirth, Transformation, and Immortality Spells

Primal Currents: Hydrocephalus Magick in the Path of Dino Wicca

The Digital Gold Rush: Mastering E-Commerce and Online Sales

Future Shock: Adapting to the Next Decade of Change

The Quantum Mindset: Think Like a Billionaire

Sacred Motherhood: Awakening the Divine Feminine Within

The Mother's Spellbook: Enchantments for Love, Protection, and Prosperity

The Witch's Guide to Parenting: Raising Empowered and Intuitive Children

The Magick of Motherhood: Reclaiming Your Power Through Rituals

The Pagan Path to Self-Love: A Goddess's Guide to Worth and Confidence

Wild Woman Magick: Unleashing Your Primal Power

The Money Magnet Blueprint: Unlocking Unlimited Wealth

Biohacking 101: Unlock Your Body's Full Potential

The Wild Father: A Pagan Guide to Strength and Wisdom

The Sacred Masculine: Unlocking Your Inner Power

The Druid's Compass

The Warrior's Mindset

The Father's Fire

Odin's Path

Ancestral Bonds

The House That Whispers

The Magician's Code

The Wild Hunt

The Green Man's Path

The Altar of Success

The Shadow and the Sword

The High Priestess's Guide to Energy Healing

The Lunar Mother

The Sacred Self-Care Grimoire

The Womb Wisdom Codex

The Wheel of the Mother

The Witch's Guide to Manifestation

The Q2 Reset
The Ultimate Guide to AI-Powered Passive Income
Escape the 9-5
AI Feline Fortunes
The Tear-Stained Grimoire
Razorblade Runes
Cemetery Sirens
The Midnight Wristwatch
The Town That Forgets
AI Horror & Creepypasta
The Hollow Frequency
The Breach Echo
The Quiet Between Worlds
The Sigil of Tharan-Khul
Summon the Vault of Y'ha'ten
The Becoming Codex
The Profit of Az'ra-nar
The Drowned Logos
Echoes of the Eldritch Will
The Deep Ledger
Necronomicon of Networth
Covenant of the Wealthwyrm
The Whisperer's Manifesto
The Rites of Azh-K'luth
The Ark of the Crawling Coin
The Tithe of Shadows
Inkheart Abyss
The Timewinds of Y'ha-nthlei
The Spiral Labyrinth of Azag-Nirrh
The Gallifreyan Heresy of the Black Pharaoh
The Psalms of Nyog-Sotha
Black Rain Alchemy
The Infinite Maw

The Entropic Blueprint
The Oracle of Sh'guul
The Book of Breach
The Drowned Saint's Testament
Dreamcraft of the Sleeper God
The Silence Market
Cthonomics: The Dark Wealth Algorithm
Invocation of the Ten-Eyed King
Wealthbound to the Wyrm Below
Become the Unnameable
Codex of the Sovereign Flame
Rituals of Relentless Becoming
The Shadow Ascends
The Eyes Beneath You
The Will That Wakes Worlds
Silence Is a Weapon
The Mirror That Screams
The Whisper Between Moments
The Mind That Devours Fear
The Myth of the Finished Self
The Architect of Your Madness
The Voice You've Buried
The Discipline of Madness
Stormborn: Awakening Your Inner Tempest
The Mind That Ate Time
Unbind Your Becoming
The Pact You Owe Yourself
The Devourer's Diet
The Acid That Carves the Path
The Tower You Must Burn
The Breath Between Worlds
Speak Like the Deep
The Labyrinth Within

The Spine of the Sea God
Rejection Is a Portal
The Crown You Refused
The Scar Is the Spell
The Lightless Flame
The Habit of Becoming Horrific
ChickenJockey Chaos
The Gatekeeper Within
You Are Not Your Name
The Compass of the Mad
The Archive of Unsent Letters
What the Mirror Can't Show You
The Knife You Needed
Worship Nothing, Become Everything
The Other Voice
The Body the World Forgot
The Vein of the Void
The Black Bone Codex
The Puzzle of the Hidden Self (Millennium Puzzle)
The Eye That Sees the Lie *(Millennium Eye)*
The Ring of Return (Millennium Ring)
The Rod of Relentless Will ***(Millennium Rod)***
The Tally of the Soul (Millennium Tauk/Necklace)
The Key to the Locked Timeline (Millennium Key)
The Scale of Sacred Decisions (Millennium Scales)
Inferno Bites: The UnOfficial Minecraft Lava Cookbook
Rot in the Attic
Prana: The Hidden Force of Your Infinite Self
The Shadow Realm Within: Transforming Darkness Into Destiny
The Borderland Collapse
Claws of Protection: Bastet's Defensive Magick
Mr. Ring-a-Ding's Madness

Yugioh Astrology: Celestial Deckcraft and Duel Destiny (2026–2027 Edition)

The Seal You Signed: Unlocking the Power You Once Feared

The Puzzle of Infinite Minds: Unlocking the Mentalism Hidden Within

The Eye That Mirrors the All: Secrets of Inner Reflection

Doctor Who: The Toymaker's Broadcast

The Rod of Eternal Flow: Commanding the Currents of Vibration

Golden Eyes of Bastet: Enhancing Psychic Vision

The Key of Dual Forces: Balance Within the Polarity

The Scales of Living Rhythm: Timing the Dance of Life

The Necklace of Hidden Cause: Weaving the Webs of Fate

The Ring of Secret Masters: Rising Through the All Within All

Daggers of the Dying Deep

Bastet's Wealth and Fortune Magick: Prosperity Rituals of the Goddess

The Tide that Speaks

The Scrolls of Petosiris: 13 Rituals from the Feathered Eye

Petosiris and the Living Plague of Osirion

Feline Fire: Bastet's Passion and Love Magick

The Star Altar of Petosiris

Bastet's Whiskers: Supernatural Sensory Magick

The Bastet Grimoire

Feeding the Shadows

The Mouthless Prayer

The Spiral Wound

Becoming the Ibis: Lessons from Petosiris's Mind

The Crimson Coven: Cola Magick for Sweet Dominion

Sacred Cat's Paw

The Soda Zodiac: A Flavor for Every Sign

Covenant of the Crawling Flame

The Ink of Ish'Zur
Frothroot: The Thirst That Ate the World
The Golden Glyphs of Prosperity
The Etherbind Codex
Echoes of the Resistance: Reclaiming the You That Survived
Harnessed Minds: Breaking Free from Mental Control
The Eyes in the Smoke
Rootwake: The Carbon Covenant
Skitter Logic: Unlearning the Fear That Built You
Doctor Who: The World That Froths
Rootwake: The Fizz That Rewrites Flesh
Rootwake: Frothfather of the World
The Holly Pact: Blood Beneath the Mistletoe
The 2nd Mass Principle: Building Unbreakable Tribes
Web of Wits: A Survival Guide to Encounters with Anasi the Spider (Aunt Nancy)
The Hexbreaking Handbook: Effective Spells to Remove Curses
Pop Alchemy: Transform Your Life One Sip at a Time
The Mason Code: Leading in Unleadable Times
Petosiris and the Fifth Chamber of Thoth
The Ether Seed Within
The Parent of Tomorrow
Petosiris's Pyramid of Perpetual Wealth
Unlearn the World
Grimoire of the Hollow Tongue
Zodiac Weeds: Finding Your Strain Through the Stars
Aquarius Rises in the Bank
The Sugar God's Smile
The Skinclock Reversal: Biohacking the Face of Time
Debtburn: How to Obliterate What You Owe Forever
The Ice Cream Oracle: What Your Cone Says About Your Future

Silence Is Sovereignty: The Power of Being Unreadable
The Wind That Whispers Through Stone
Path of the Four Directions
Doctor Who: The Maestro's Symphony of Endings
Oxygen Grail: Breathing to Undo the Clock
Zodiacal Collapse: When Stars Devour Time
Teachings from the Red Sand Silence
Doctor Who: Omega – The Broken Equation
Memory Wipe Your Past: Start Over Like a MiB
Mitochondria Prime: Ignite the Core of Youth
A Nest of Roaches
Grub from the Galaxy: MiB Recipes You'll Never Forget
Whiskers of Power: Bastet's Guide to Inner Sovereignty
The Gift Must Cost Them: Negotiation Through Unequal Exchange
The Worm Guys' Wealth Code: Hustle Like an Alien
Bug Out: The Edgar Method for Ruthless Goal Setting
Weaving Life with Spiderwoman's Pattern
Doctor Who: The Rani's Renaissance
How to Get a Job (If You're a Puppygirl)
Speak Through Others: The Art of Proxy Power
T-Rex Your Trauma: Reclaim the Power of Your Primal Self
The Black Briefcase: How MiB Stay Wealthy in Silence
The Thirst Beyond Reason: Understanding Diabetes Insipidus From the Inside Out
Backwoods Witchcraft for Billionaires: The Pagan Path from Dirt Roads to Gold Roads
The Moonshine Grimoire: Fermented Spells for Abundance
The Nameless Geometry
The Wraith's Mixtape: Spellcasting with Songs of Sorrow
The Gallifreyan Gentleman: Silent Wealth, Sonic Confidence, and the Doctor's Code of Living

Sugar Water Confidence
Dino Totems: Spirit Guides from Earth's First Gods
Pumpkin Sigils & Ritual Smoke
The Hózhó Compass
The Distortus Discipline – Order from Inner Mutation
Witchcraft for the Cold-Blooded Soul
Moonlight Over the Blessingway
Water, Interrupted: When the Body Forgets How to Hold On
Deformed but Divine: Embracing Your Asymmetry
Hexes in the Henhouse: The Farm Witch's Guide to Power
The Reversed Flame: A Grimoire of Inverted Power
Salt, Cells, and Sanity: Reclaiming Balance with Diabetes Insipidus
King of the Broken: Crowning the Flawed Self
Moonlight Scars: Emo Moon Magick and the Art of Lunar Sorrow
Noose Spells: Magick of the Hanging Rope
The Goth Cathedral: Rituals of the Broken and Beautiful
The Cretaceous Codex: Dino Spirits and Fossil Magick
The Turkey Bones Ritual
Nine Lives of Manifestation: Unlocking Bastet's Reality Codes
Chaos Muscles: Building Strength from Twisted Pain
Emo Blood Magick: The Veins of Power
The 3AM Flood: Nighttime Urination, Sleep Loss, and the DI Spiral
The Silence Between the Stars
The Lemon Method: Sour Your Way to Success
Starlit Sovereign
The Rite of Twelve Gates: Walking the Gates of the Duat.
Cornbread and Conjure: Recipes for Riches and Rootwork
The Black Rose Rituals: Emo Love Spells and Obsession Magick
The Eternal Goodbye: Death Magick and Rebirth Rituals

Sinkrot: The Drain That Remembers
The Hybrid Mindset: Thinking Beyond Evolution
Bone Dry: Navigating Dehydration Before It Breaks You
Wreathcraft: Winter Sigils and Yuletide Spells
The Rite of Twelve Mouths
S'mores of the Damned: Haunted Recipes for Halloween Night
Rethink the Drink: A Beverage Survival Guide for DI Warriors
The Shadow Chord: Guitar Magick and Sonic
Malformed Yet Majestic: Leading When You Feel Wrong Inside
The Cursed Diary: Ink-Stained Spells of the Emo Soul
Anxiety Off Switch: Emergency Reset for a Fried Nervous System
The Energy Heist: How to Take Back Your Life from Drainers
Beyond the Bathroom: Rebuilding Your Social Life With DI
Coyote's Gift for Decision Makers
Ghoul-Goo: Spooky S'mores You'll Die For
Echoes in the Mirror: Scrying and Self-Destruction Magick
Thread and Thorn: Stitching Spells from Rural Cloth
The Mogwai Mind: Building Untouchable Wealth from Small Ideas
Be Your Own Guide: Trust Your Inner Compass
Hormones in Chaos: The Endocrine Puzzle of Diabetes Insipidus
ChronoCleanse: Detox Your Biological Timeline
The Limb You Hide Is the One That Saves You
Leaves, Bones, and Whisper Spells
The Dinosaur Mindset: Prehistoric Tactics for Modern Wealth
Clawing Back Control: A Bastet Method for Boundaries and Empowerment

Samhain Codes of the Forgotten
Orange Alchemy: The Autumnal Spellbook
Monster Within, Master Without
The Sigil That Sleeps
Hearthcraft: Yule Hearth Sigils and Winter Warmth Spells
Temple of the Purring Moon: Rituals from Bastet's Lineage
When the Earth Remembers Your Footsteps
Food for Mood: Eat to Heal Depression, Not Just Survive It
Witch of the Kudzu Vine: Southern Pagan Wealth Secrets
The Invisible Diagnosis: Advocating for Yourself With DI
The Coffin's Lullaby: Sleep Magick and Nightmares as Portals
Ashes of the Will: Rituals for Erasing the Self
The Fracture Rite: Shattering the Magickal Core
Funeral Candles: The Art of Emo Flame Magick
The Black Grimoire: A Blank Ritual for Writing in Absence
Phantom Thirst: A Halloween Survival Guide for Diabetes Insipidus
The Hollow Crown: Emo Royalty and Magick of the Outcast King
Sandpainting for the Soul
Falling Into Balance: Using the Extra Hour to Recalibrate Life
100 Southern Superstitions That Still Work
The DI Child: A Parent's Guide to Raising Hydrated, Happy Kids
The Jungle of Shame: Escaping the Hidden Lab of Doubt
The Witch's Toast: S'mores Spells and Creepy Confections
The Hoodoo Pantry: Spells from the Mason Jar
The Immortal Fortune: Secret Wealth Lessons from Captain Jack Harkness
The Specter's Embrace: Magick for Channeling Ghostly Lovers
Grateful Waters: A Thanksgiving Survival Guide for Diabetes Insipidus

The Seizure Gospel

Harvestbind: Autumn Sigils and Samhain Spells

Doctor Who: The Algorithmic Awakening

Silent Nights, Steady Waters: A Christmas Survival Guide for Diabetes Insipidus

The Extra Hour Effect: How One Hour Can Transform Everything

Blade Between the Breaths

Running with the Mountain Shadows

Echoes of the Failed Experiment – Becoming a Living Legacy

Swamp Witches & River Ghosts: Real Southern Hauntings

Cornbread Prophecies: Magical Recipes from a Southern Table

Doctor Who: The Signal in the Star

Bloomcraft: Spring Sigils and Equinox Enchantments

Vanisher: How to Disappear from the Internet Without Losing Your Life

The Ultimate Christmas Cookie Cookbook

The Unbreakable Parent: How to Mentally Survive Raising Kids in a Broken World

Time Debt: How to Reclaim the Hours You Didn't Know You Lost

One Month, One Million: Unconventional Cash Creation Tactics

Doctor Who: The Cyber Conversion Protocol

Black Friday Frenzy: The Art of Finding Hidden Online Deals

The Grimoire Buried Under the Apple Tree

Digital Couponing Masterclass: Your Step-by-Step Guide to Black Friday Savings

The Fire Inside the Flint

Shadows on the Ceiling: The Emo Guide to Astral Magick

The Bone-Eaters Beneath Us

Black Friday Bundle Blueprint: Creating Irresistible Product Packages for Maximum Sales

Thirteen Nights of Unbinding

Doctor Who: Engines of Influence

Pumpkin Spice Alchemy: Recipes of Fire and Frost

When Raptor Met Rexy: Prehistoric Lessons in Wild Romance

Oblivion's Candle: Burn the Path Behind You

Campfire Curses and Chocolate: A Halloween S'mores Grimoire

The Wallet That Wasn't Mine: Breaking Free from Inherited Scarcity

The Cola Zodiac: What Your Fizz Says About Your Fate

Frostfire Fortune: Unlocking Winter's Hidden Prosperity

Signal Jamming: Detox Your Brain from Info Overload

The Dust of the Forgotten Rite

The Golden Cat Sigils: Drawing Power in Bastet's Name

Mud Magick: The Prosperity of Getting Dirty

Savory Spicefall: Beyond the Pumpkin Pie

Pumpkin Spice Apothecary Kitchen

The Pumpkin Spice Economy: Turning Trends into Billions

The Ember Veil: 13 Nights of Fire Magick

Financial Freeze: When Earning Triggers Panic

The Gingerbread Alchemist: Sweet Recipes with a Twist

Biosynth Power: Programming Yourself from Scratch

Echoes from the Talking Circle

Truffle Alchemy: Fungus of Fortune

Spores of Power: The Truffle Witch's Handbook

Doctor Who: The Tower That Speaks

The Mycelium Veil: Truffle Magick Unbound

Broke But Ashamed: Healing the Shame Wound of Debt

The Evergreen Mind: Growth Through Winter Stillness

The Black Veil Truffle Rite

The Voice Beneath Symbols
Witchlight on the Bayou: Swamp Spells for Sovereignty
I Grew Up Poor and Now I Sabotage My Success
The Lantern of Hollow Souls
Shutdown Survival: A Citizen's Guide to Thriving When Government Stops
When Abundance Feels Like a Threat: Healing the Hidden Fears of Enough
The Scarecrow Grimoire
Owls of the October Veil
Candlewax and Curses: A Halloween Spellbook
Excavating the Inner Fossil – Transforming Fossilized Thoughtforms into Tools of Power
The Yule Witch's Spellbook: Magick for the Holiday Season
Haunted Christmas: Ghost Stories for Winter Nights
The Christmas Survival Guide: Thriving Through the Chaos
The Bone Orchard Rites
Haunted Commerce: The Ghost in the Marketplace
When Money Triggers the Inner Child
Silent Night with the Silence: A Christmas Thriller
The Lightning Crown: Living and Leading Through Seizures
TARDIS Tidings: Festive Stories from the Whoniverse
Autumn Reset: Slowing Down Without Falling Behind
The Trillion Dollar Soul: Rewriting the Currency of Reality
Truffle Eclipse Magick
Micro-Manifestations: Quick Magick That Works
5-Minute Rituals for Busy Witches
The Marshmallow Massacre: Halloween Treats with a Sinister Twist
Blood and Blackberry Thorns
Magickal Mornings: Rituals for a Blessed Christmas Day
Embers of the All-Hallows Fire
The Pumpkin Market Collapse

The Hour You Gained: Transforming Time Into Power

The Chamber Must Be Sealed: Mastering the Power of Controlled Access

The Cursed Manuscript of Petosiris

The Festive Hearth: Creating Holiday Traditions

Darkness Rising: Thriving as Nights Grow Longer

Harvesting Time: Turning the Year's End Into Your New Beginning

Petosiris and the 13th Zodiac Key

Wagewound: When Paychecks Become Identity Prisons

Walls That Watch

The Silent Feast: Rituals of Power in the Longest Night

The Distortus Legacy : Becoming a Deformed King in a Perfect World

The Hollow Masks

The Gratitude Furnace: Forging Gold from Thanks

Feast of Inner Gold: Eating for Energy and Enlightenment

Haunted Commerce: The Season of Spending Spirits

Fear Bonds: How Panic Creates Profit

Black Friday E-Commerce Playbook: Sales Tactics to Skyrocket Your Holiday Revenue

Budgeting for Black Friday: A Holiday Savings Planner

Haunting the Harvest Moon

The Warrior's Water: Emergency Preparedness for People With DI

The First Sip of the Year: A New Year's Survival Guide for Diabetes Insipidus

Doctor Who: The Thirteenth Node

The Unseen Struggle: Mental Health, Anxiety, and Chronic Thirst

The Hearth's Hidden Ledger: Counting Energies as Currency

The Gift Alchemist: Turning Any Offering Into Gold

The Papyrus of the Bound Spirit

The Magick of Leftovers: Transmutation in the Fridge

Frost and Fortune: Christmas Wealthcraft for the Modern Magus

Last-Minute Gifts: Creative Ideas on a Budget

10 Secrets to Surviving Holiday Crowds

The Witch's Dow Jones

The Witches' Graveyard Shift

Pumpkin Sigils: Carving Rites for Midnight Power

The Secret Shopper's Black Friday Guide: How to Get Early Access and VIP Deals

Fever in the Foundation

The Neuralyzer Reset: Reprogram Your Morning Routine

Lightning Lessons of the White Painted Woman

The Enchanted Snowflake

The Magic Sip: Surviving Disney Parks with Diabetes Insipidus

The One Who Draws Through You

Santa's Secrets: A Magical Holiday Planner

Silent Bells, Loud Miracles: Self-Help for the Season of Stillness

The Sugar Spell Codex: Confectionary Magick of Christmas

Autumn Hexcraft: Fallen Leaves, Fallen Barriers

Sleep Like a Fortress: Build a Life Where Insomnia Can't Survive

Nowhere Was Ever Home

Christmas Under the Stars: A Celestial Holiday Guide

Rentproof: How to Never Be Evicted Again

Workless: Escape the 9-5 Without Being Broke

The Gilded Gift: A Wealth Altar for Christmas Morning

The Black Friday Grimoire

The Hollowing: Ceremonies of Spiritual Collapse

Doctor Who: The Nameless Signal

Where the Eagle Hides His Courage

The Dwarf Tyrant's Ascent: Claiming Power in a World of Giants

The Currency of the Dead: Trading with Spectral Bankers

The Icebound Witch: Survival and Magick in the Cold

The Emergency Money Mind: Constant Crisis, Zero Calm

Thirst & Roses: A Valentine's Survival Guide for Diabetes Insipidus

Springing Into Clarity: Mastering the Energy Shift of Daylight Saving

Speed of the Nanotyrant: Agile Strategies for Life's Hunt

The 90-Day Reset: A Science-Backed Guide to Reinvent Yourself Before the New Year

The Coil of Thorns

Timegates Unleashed

Dopamine Fasting 2.0: Rewiring Your Brain in a World of Overstimulation

The Nanotyrannus Mutation: Embracing Your Differentiated Form

Unwritten January: How to Use the Blank Page of the Year to Re-Author Your Life

Feast of the Forgotten Spirits: Ancestor Magick for the Holidays

The Burnout Codex: A System for Thriving Beyond Stress

I Don't Deserve to Have Money

When the King Doesn't See You: The Shadow Predator's Guide

The Reset Ritual :A Guide to Shedding Last Year's Weight—Emotional and Physical—by Spring Cleaning Your Soul

Calendar Alchemy: Learn to Bend Time and Productivity around Your Natural Rhythms

The Mirror Contract: A One-Sentence Agreement with Yourself that Unlocks Real Change

The Nile Formula: Sacred Flow for Millionaire Minds

Forward Momentum: Productivity Rituals for the Lost Hour
Harvest Gold: Wealth Magick of Pumpkin Spice Commerce
The Magick of Christmas Lights: Illuminating Holiday Rituals
Cranberry Crown: Royal Self-Worth through Ritual Meals
Petosiris and the Worms of the Feathered Throne
The Evergreen Equation: Self-Help for Sustained Growth
The Rain Will Wash Us Away: Emo Weather Magick
Snowlight Shadows: Magick Under Frozen Stars
Doctor Who: Merger of Empires
The Light Within the Feast: Magickal Wealth of Yuletide Flame
Momentum Machines: Small Habits Designed to Snowball into Unstoppable Forward Motion
Calm Spells: Magickal Solutions for Anxiety Relief
Santa's Final List: The Naughty Never Leave
The Mystic's Guide to Banishing Worry
The Silence Dividend: Turning Quiet Mornings into Compounding Growth All Year
Charmed Stillness: Rituals to Ease the Mind
Blood Spiral Ascension
The Vanishing Heart Invocation
Crystal Calm: Harnessing Stones for Anxiety
The Nano Tyrant Code: Strength in the Small Predator
The Energy Ledger: Accounting Methods for Vitality, Not Just Money
Snowglobe Mindset: Shake Up Your Thoughts, Settle Into Peace
The Weight of the Feather: Anubis's Codes for Soul Balance
Pocket Peppermint Power: Tiny Rituals for Big Holiday Energy
Shadowkeeper of the Golden Jackal: Anubis's Path to Energetic Protection

The Tenth Doctor: The Lonely Hero (David Tennant, 2005–2010)

The Eleventh Doctor: The Madman in a Box (Matt Smith, 2010–2013)

The Twelfth Doctor: The Rebel with a Cause (Peter Capaldi, 2013–2017)

The Thirteenth Doctor: Breaking the Mold
(Jodie Whittaker, 2017–2022)

The Fourteenth Doctor: A New Beginning (David Tennant, 2022–2023)

The Fifteenth Doctor: Rewriting the Stars
(Ncuti Gatwa, 2023–2025)

Santa's Shortcut to Success: Micro Habits for a Better New Year

The Midnight Cocoa Manifesto: Comfort Rituals for Hard Nights

Why I Can't Save: Trauma Blocks to Financial Planning

Dino Brain, Mega Goals: Rewire Yourself for Savage Success.

Jurassic Profit: Unearth Your Inner Millionaire Fossil

Scales & Softness: Dating with Dino Heart

Carnotaurus Dreams.

Red Willow Thinking.

Reindeer Resilience: How to Keep Going When You're Exhausted

Candlewick Courage: Lighting Strength in Dark Seasons.

Elf-Mode Focus: Fast Attention Fixes for Busy Seasons

Futureproof Feelings: Emotional Skill-Building for Resilience No Matter What the New Year Brings

The 90-Day Rewire: Transform Your Neural Pathways Before Spring Blooms

Jolly Rich: Christmas Micro-Money Magick for Fast Prosperity.

Gingerbread Gratitude: Mini Practices for a Happier Holiday

Trauma-Spending: When Money Becomes a Drug

Goal Skeletons: Build Minimalist Frameworks for Resolutions That Last

The Snarl Strategy: Growling Back at a World That Silenced You

The Hourglass Reset: Reclaiming What the Clock Took

Yule Claw: Dino Rites of Light in the Darkness

Sacred Circles: Grounding Rituals for Anxious Souls

Clockstopper's Gut: Rebuilding the Core of Time

Winterfire Drive: Harness the Cold Season's Stillness to Ignite Deep Motivation

The 5-Minute Productivity Hack: Small Steps to Big Results

Light Ascending: A Self-Help Guide to Longer Days

Inner Economy: Trade Self-Doubt for Confidence Like a High-Value Currency

Simple Success: Decluttering Your Life for Better Results

The Resilient Mind: Thriving in Tough Times

The 2026 Playbook: Mastering the Year Ahead

The Spring Sleep Solution: Conquering Fatigue After Time Change.

The Hormonal Compass: Navigate Back to Your Youth

Golden Vision: Eating for Your Eye Color with the Power of Ghee

Lionhearted Love: Strength in Relationships

MiB Mindset: Think Like a Cosmic Agent

The Ladder of Small Wins: Climb Out of Stagnation by Stacking Micro-Victories

The Momentum Hour: Gaining More in Less Time.

The Year of You: A Self-Help Blueprint for Unapologetic Self-Ownership

The Dust That Watches You Back.

The Astral Parent

Shadow of the King: The Nanotyrannus Parable

Tiny Tidings of Triumph: Small Wins That Change Your Life

Dwarf Tyrant Rising: When You're the One They Overlook

The Bank Account Mirror: Healing How You See Yourself Through Money

Cretaceous Black

When Love Costs Too Much: Romantic Triggers and Financial Wounds

Dream-Eater's Guide to Wealth

Unzipped Reality: The Jacket That Opens Portals

The Power of No: How to Set Boundaries and Get Rich

Keeper of the Desert Veil: Anubis's Teachings on Illusion & Truth

Redacted Stargates: Stories the SGC Buried

The Clock That Dripped Time

Doctor Who: The Silent Acquisition

Hairline Manifestation: Unlocking Power at the Edge of Thought

Cash-Eater Crickets: How Insects Predict Economic Collapse

Dead Pet Whisperer: Grief Alchemy from the Other Side

The Love Algorithm Is Broken: Hack Romance Before It Hacks You

The Rite of the 8-Limbed Seal

Melt the Moon: A Fire Ritual to Reshape Emotion

Venomous Miracles: Healing Through the Poison Path

Wealth Without Water: The Post-Aquatic Rich Life

The Butterfly Betrayal: When Change Turns on You

The Quiet Upgrade: How Humans Are Secretly Rebuilding Themselves Without Asking Permission

Nobody Taught Us This: The Missing Human Manual for Money, Energy, and Self-Respect

You Were Never Broken: Why Most People Are Reacting Normally to an Unstable World

After the Noise Ends: How Humans Reset When the World Finally Goes Quiet

The Month That Tells the Truth: Why January Reveals What the Rest of the Year Hides

Tremors Party Unleashed: The Ultimate Guide to a Graboids Birthday Bash

Cold Start Human: Rebooting Motivation Without Forcing Momentum

The Year that doesn't start until they say

Love Without Performance: What Connection Looks Like When No One Is Watching

February Is a Mirror: What Love Exposes About You

How We Learned Love Wrong: Uninstalling Cultural Myths About Connection

You Are Not Too Much: Why Needing Love Is Not a Flaw

The Crooked Fence Covenant: Backwoods Boundaries and Witch Wealth

The Day That Keeps Repeating: Why Your Life Feels Stuck—and How to Shift It Gently

Nothing Changes Until Something Softens: Escaping Repetition Without Violence to Yourself

Same Life, Different Ending: How Tiny Choices Rewrite Repetition

The Loop Isn't Punishment: Why You're Being Asked to Learn, Not Suffer

Panic at the Register: Retail Anxiety and Public Shame

The Secret Formula to Becoming an Influencer in 90 Days

The New Rich: How to Retire by 35

Digital Nomad Secrets: How to Travel the World and Make Millions

Burn Your Waiting Room: Escape the Delay Spiral

Strapped for Pleasure: A Complete Guide to Pegging and Strap-On Play

Locked in Desire: A Guide to Chastity Play and Intimate Control

Burrowing into History: Groundhog Day Through the Ages

The Shadow Forecast: The Science of Groundhog Day

Choice Cascades: How One Decision in January Sets Ripples for the Whole Year

The Anti-Anxiety Blueprint: Mastering Fear and Stress for Success

The Ancestral Path of the Jackal Priest

Winterborn Titans: Giants of Ice and Stone

The Extinction Spire

The Emotion That Made Me Millions

Delete Their Voice: Become Unreachable

The Frostbound Mysteries: Mythical Beings of January's Chill

The Roar Within: Unlocking Your Potential

From Burrow to Sky: Groundhog Day Explained

The Boogey Book: Festive Ward-Off Edition

Fooled Ya! The Psychology Behind Great Pranks

April Fools' Alchemy: Transforming Everyday Items into Pranks

Anchor Habits: Root Yourself in Unshakable Routines That Endure Seasonal Change

Emerald Waters: A St. Patrick's Day Survival Guide for Diabetes Insipidus

The Groundhog's Legacy: Myths, Legends, and Facts

Six Weeks of Mystery: The Truth Behind Groundhog Day

The Upgrade Mind: Tech-Like Patches and Updates for Your Mental Operating System

Moon Blood, Star Flesh: Embracing Your Hybrid Nature

Groundhog Lore and Legend: A Complete Guide

You Are the Lie They Can't Kill

Download a Different Reality

The Quiet Advantage: Winning Without Announcing Yourself

A Year of Gratitude: Unlocking Joy

Touch Grass: A Pagan Reset for a Burned-Out Digital World

Cold Start Wealth: Building Financial Power from a Standing Still Point

Astrology Without Fate: Using Cycles Without Surrendering Control

The Future is Remote: Work Less, Earn More, Live Anywhere

Harvest of Silence

The Algorithm Knows Your Name

April Fools' Day for Introverts

Soft Power Systems: Influence That Doesn't Exhaust You

Practical Magick for Real Life: Focus, Intent, and Follow-Through

January Is a Lie: Designing Momentum Without the Calendar

Universal Flow: Managing DI in High-Energy Theme Parks

Electric Allure: Exploring Erotic Electro-Play

The Masked Embrace: Exploring Sensory Deprivation

The Ultimate April Fools' Survival Guide

Splashproof Survival: Waterparks & Wave Pools with DI

Agile Predator, Still King: Crafting Your Speed in a World That Celebrates Size

The Shadow Feast: Groundhog Day's Sinister Side

The Bug's Business Model

Edge of Bliss: Mastering the Art of Tease and Denial

Midnight Alchemy: Rituals for Transformation Between the Old Year and the New

Punxsutawney Bloodlines: A Groundhog Day Horror

The Burrower: Groundhog Day's Darkest Secrets

Buried Alive: A Groundhog Day Horror Story

Blood Moon Markets: The Witch's Guide to Wealth Magick

The Groundhog's Shadow: What It Means for the World

Seasonal Shadows: The Groundhog Day Phenomenon
The Shadow's Curse: A Groundhog Day Horror Tale
Punxsutawney Revealed: A Guide to Groundhog Day
Safari Hydration: Zoo & Wildlife Park Survival for DI
The Foolproof Prank Planner
***Latex Lust: Embracing Fetish Fashion* is a sophisticated**
Whip & Whisper: The Dynamics of Impact Play
The Shadow Burrow Chronicles: Horror Beneath the Ground
Frozen Shadows: A Groundhog Day Thriller
The Groundhog's Revenge: A February Nightmare
Burrow of the Damned
Everyday Enchantment: Magickal Practices for Modern Living
Budget Bliss: The Easy Path to Financial Freedom
Six More Weeks of Terror
The Oxygen Debt
The Ice Veil: Mystical Beasts of January's Shadows
Roots That Remember
Polar Myths: Creatures of the Icy Abyss
The Marginalia Covenant
AI and the Occult: Digital Spirits, Sigils, and Cyber-Witchcraft
Roleplay Realms: Crafting Fantasies and Scenes
The Last Clean River
Lover in the Shadows: A Groundhog Day Tale
Buried Hearts: A Groundhog Day Gothic Romance
Anubis Wept for Petosiris
The Lantern Knows Your Name
Rituals of the Last Shadow
The Bell That Rings for No One
Shadows of Love and Death
The Groundhog's Bride: A Dark Valentine's Tale
Frozen Kisses: A Horror Romance for Groundhog Day
The Creative Spark: Igniting Your Passion Projects

From Cub to King: A Journey of Transformation
Six Weeks to Midnight: A Groundhog Day Romance
Tide of the Unclean
Burrow of Desire: A Groundhog Day Paranormal Romance
The Shadow Magick Almanac: Harnessing Groundhog Day Energies
AI for Emo Influencers: Growing an Online Following Without the Anxiety
AI for the Melancholy Millionaire: Making Money Without Social Interaction
Winter's Grip: A Horror Romance Beneath the Frost
Shadowed Hearts: A Love Buried in Winter's Chill
The Shadow Lover: A Groundhog Day Gothic Love Story
Beneath the Burrow: A Groundhog Day Thriller
The Punxsutawney Conspiracy
The Crimson Pact: Emo Blood Oath Magick
The Shadows of Gallifrey: A Doctor Who Horror Collection
Whispers in the Vortex: Chilling Tales from the TARDIS
AI Ghostwriting for Emo Souls: How to Make Money Writing Without Trying
The Anti-Social Emo's Guide to AI-Powered Freelancing
Emo AI Therapy: Talking to Robots When Humans Suck
Cry & Collect: AI-Powered Passive Income for Emos
The Weeping Angel Chronicles: A Collection of Terror
Dating Without the Mask
The Clockwork Menace: Horror Stories from the Future
Tender Doesn't Mean Weak
Not a Burden, Not a Bonus
Dalek Nightmares: Stories of Ultimate Extermination
The Empty Child's Curse: Tales of Horror and Fear
The TARDIS Ghost Files: Hauntings Across the Universe
Soft Armor, Open Heart
Chosen Gently

Love That Doesn't Rush You

Financial Gaslighting: When You're Made to Feel Crazy About Money.

After the Bees Went Silent

The Soil Knows Your Name

The Quantum Magick Codex: Unlocking the Hidden Laws of Reality

The Gingerbread Golem's Awakening: A Tale of Sweet Revenge

The Gingerbread Golem Chronicles: Guardians of Frost Hollow

The Power of Focus: Eliminate Distractions, Achieve Greatness

Sacred Submission: The Dynamics of D/s Relationships

The Magick of Numbers: Unlocking the Hidden Codes of the Universe

Blood and Bones: The Ancient Magick of Life and Death

Doctor Who: The Collapse Dividend

Thesis of the Unremembered

Desired as You Are

The Energy Budget of Love

Romancing Your Potential: The Love Month Growth Guide

Seen, Not Studied

Screams from the Void: Horror Stories Inspired by Doctor Who

The Silence Is Watching: A Collection of Dread

Under the Floorboards

The House of Feathers and Fangs

Emperor Bones, Hollow Crown

Goreglyphs of the Boiling Deep

The Coven That Screamed Back

The Stacks That Breathe

Love That Adapts

Nightmares on Gallifrey: Frights from the Doctor Who Universe

Apache Ways to Heal Powerfully

Belos Left No Corpses

The Algorithm Hates You (Good.)

Starve the Soul, Feed the Flame

Romance Without Apology

The Carbon Illusion

Your Nervous System is Your GPS

Where Rest Learns Your Name: Six Gentle Bedtime Stories for Minds That Work Differently

Soft Armor for Tender Nights: Six 5-Minute Bedtime Stories for Hearts That Have Been Hurt

Paws of Night, Path of Stars: Six 5-Minute Bedtime Stories Guided by Bastet and Anubis

When the Mind Needs a Lamp: Six 5-Minute Bedtime Stories for Gentle Mental Health Care

Imbolc Roar: Awakening the Dino Flame

The Titan Never Died

Witchflesh Harvest

Become the Thought They Can't Unsee

Golden Threads: The Sensuality of Body Worship

Chains of Desire: Exploring the Beauty of Restraint

Glyphs Written in Organs

Living Below the Line

Palismen Don't Scream—Until They Do

The Boiling Isles Devour the Weak

Hexside Anatomy Lab

Philip Wittebane and the First Body

Money PTSD: When Trauma Hijacks Your Finances

Brother, Bone, and Betrayal

Lipstick Like a Weapon: A Goth Girl's Guide to Emotional Dominance, Boundaries, and Quiet Intimidation

The Scar Is the Portal
Don't Grow—Mutate

www.ingramcontent.com/pod-product-compliance
Lightning Source LLC
LaVergne TN
LVHW022007200926
848481LV00007B/2275
9798295607684